Gr...
Books
—❧ *of the* ❧—
Christian
Tradition

TERRY W. GLASPEY

HARVEST HOUSE PUBLISHERS
Eugene, Oregon 97402

The author may be contacted c/o Harvest House Publishers, 1075 Arrowsmith, Eugene, OR 97402

Except where otherwise indicated, Scripture quotations in this book are taken from the Holy Bible, New International Version®, Copyright © 1973, 1978, 1984 by the International Bible Society. Used by permission of Zondervan Publishing House. The "NIV" and "New International Version" trademarks are registered in the United States Patent and Trademark Office by International Bible Society.

GREAT BOOKS OF THE CHRISTIAN TRADITION
Copyright © 1996 by Harvest House Publishers
Eugene, Oregon 97402

Library of Congress Cataloging-in-Publication Data
Glaspey, Terry W.
    Great books of the Christian tradition / Terry Glaspey.
        p.   cm.
    ISBN 1-56507-356-9 (alk. paper)
    1. Bibliography—Best books—Christianity.   2. Christian literature—
Abstracts.   3. Theology—Abstracts.   I. Title.
Z7751.G55   1996
[BR117]
016.2—dc20   95-34307
                                                                        CIP

Printed in the United States of America.

    97 98 99 00 01 - 10 9 8 7 6 5 4 3 2

To the members of
The Frugal Chariot,
in appreciation for
much laughter, insight,
and inspiration.
"See you next month."

Thanks . . .

To Sally Glaspey, for editorial insight, constructive criticism, and putting up with my long hours at the keyboard. To Emma and Kathryn, who enjoyed many of the children's classics with me. I am blessed with such a wonderful family.

To Mortimer Adler and Clifton Fadiman, whose writings introduced me to the joys of great books.

To Jay and Julia Moore and the crew at Thin Air, for all their hard work on the self-published earlier edition of this volume. Thanks for having the vision to see that this list really could be a book!

To all who offered encouragement and enthusiasm for this project, especially Dean and Karen Andreola, Ranell Curl, Michael Bailey, Lori Stone, and Kathi MacKenzie-Foster.

To all my friends at Harvest House, most especially Carolyn McCready, Betty Fletcher, and Steve Miller. Your ideas and insights have been most helpful.

Contents

The Power
of Books

L et me begin with a heartfelt confession.

I admit it. I am a biblioholic, one who loves books and whose life would seem incomplete without them. I am an addict, with a compulsive need to stop by nearly any bookstore I pass in order to get my fix. For me, reading is one of the most enjoyable ways to pass a rainy afternoon. I crave the knowledge and insights that truly great books bring into my life, and I can spend transported hours scouring used book stores for volumes which "I simply must have." I love the smell and feel of well-loved books and the look of a bookcase full of books waiting to be taken down and read.

My love of reading came into my life at about the same time as my conversion. I had a hunger to learn more about the faith I had newly embraced, so I began to read just about everything I could get my hands on: biographies of famous Christians, both past and present, books explaining and defending Christian doctrine, books on deepening the spiritual life, and books that elucidated the meaning of the greatest of all books, the Bible. At that time, my search for understanding and learning seemed unquenchable. To be honest, it still does. If you make it a goal in life to constantly keep your mind open to new ideas and to better understand the beliefs and values you already hold, then books become a necessary companion on the journey of life. God Himself chose the medium of a book as His primary way to communicate to us the truth of His love and grace. The life of Christ is forever revealed and offered to us in the medium of a book.

When we ponder church history, we find that many great leaders and thinkers were set on their path through the agency of a book which transformed their life or their way of thinking.

♦♦♦

The writings of Augustine helped a young monk named Martin Luther, who was struggling with the weight of his sin and his inability to gain the confidence that God had forgiven him. Augustine enlightened Luther's study of the book of Romans and opened him up to a new understanding of the meaning of grace, faith, and salvation. Augustine's books helped Martin Luther to clarify and solidify his understanding of justification by faith alone. In turn, Luther used pamphlets and books to spread the message of the Reformation.

♦♦♦

The origins of the Pietist movement, which brought about much-needed revival to the church, were not linked to a mass movement, a memorable speech, or a heart-stirring sermon, but rather to a small book (less than 70 pages) entitled *Pia Desideria.* This book was a call to church reformation and renewal and pointed people to a return to a biblical and holy church. Its message spread quickly to Christians all over Europe, and its impact is almost inestimable.

♦♦♦

John Wesley, the founder of Methodism, knew the power and influence of books. He was himself a prolific writer, the author of numerous books. Besides his own influential writings, he gathered together excerpts from the great Christian classics for use in training Methodist preachers. The early Methodist preachers were circuit riders who covered much territory on horseback, bringing the gospel to far-separated congregations. It is said that these preachers carried two saddlebags with them: one for clothes and one for the books which they distributed to their fellow believers. Wesley himself was a voracious reader. He covered untold miles on horseback, riding without the reins so that he might read while he rode. Concerned that he might fall off his horse and hurt himself, some friends eventually provided him with a carriage. His first step was to have a bookcase built into it. This carriage not only provided more solitude for reading, but was also much safer!

◆◆◆

John Newton was the captain of a slave ship that transported human cargo across the seas. It was the experience of reading *The Imitation of Christ* by Thomas à Kempis that changed his life and caused him to disown his inhuman occupation. Newton became a minister, and is best known to us today as the author of the hymn "Amazing Grace." Similarly, it was a book by Philip Doddridge that awakened the soul and the conscience of Englishman William Wilberforce, who led the fight against the slave trade in England.

◆◆◆

Nearer our own time, C. S. Lewis counted the reading of G. K. Chesterton's *Everlasting Man* and George MacDonald's *Phantastes* as key moments in his own pilgrimage toward faith. Lewis's own book *Mere Christianity* has played a major role in the lives of many searchers after the truth, including former presidential counsel Charles Colson.

Books have always been powerful tools in awakening hearts, minds, and consciences. Almost without exception, those men and women whom God has used most powerfully were men and women who knew the value of good books.

It is the same for us today. Through the medium of great books we can be expanded, transformed, informed, and spiritually enlightened. Some of the most life-changing experiences in my own life came about through certain books, which seemed to bring just the message I needed to hear at key junctures in my life. I can promise you that time spent with some of the great books introduced in this volume will bring you to a deeper awareness of the truths of God and the realities of the human existence.

1

Discovering
Our Christian
Heritage

The only palliative [for the errors of our modern world] is to keep the clean sea breeze of the centuries blowing through our minds, and this can be done only by reading old books. Not, of course, that there is any magic about the past. People were no cleverer than they are now; they made as many mistakes as we. But not the same mistakes.

—C.S. LEWIS

All the glory of the world would be buried in oblivion, unless God had provided mortals with the remedy of books.

—RICHARD DE BURY

When Sharon entered college, she was a bright and enthusiastic Christian. Four years later, her faith was more timid and less self-assured. Though she still hung on to the emotional comforts of her faith, she had given up trying to integrate her faith with her intellectual pursuits. In the world of academia, her belief system seemed somehow irrelevant and old-fashioned. Her evangelical commitment was, her professors told her, just one of many options in terms of an intellectual framework.

What Sharon had failed to understand before she entered college is that the Christian faith is not just some unique modern way of looking at life, but the single most powerful influence in the construction of Western civilization. Her professors failed to point out the vital impact of a personal faith on innumerable artists, writers, and thinkers, and that Christianity is not just a conservative fad, but a richly textured way of looking at life and understanding our human existence. Sharon, like many other Christian young people, had become intellectually embarrassed of her faith, but this embarrassment arose primarily through her lack of awareness of just how rich and diverse the Christian tradition really is. An awareness of our heritage as believers gives us a sense of confidence and pride in the face of a secularism that dismisses our faith as an empty, passing fad.

Our imaginations are not nourished by an exclusive diet of the new. The growth of the moral imagination requires us to partake of the rich feast of the past. This goes against the grain of modern thinking. Tradition has a bad name in our society, and often in evangelical circles as well. When many people think of tradition, they think of a mindless following of old and antiquated ways. They see it as an exterminator of spontaneity, a shallow and lifeless substitution of yesterday's belief for today's practice. I do not believe that this does justice to the biblical view, which stresses the importance of handing down the riches of our faith. To teach our children to appreciate our Christian heritage and to drink deeply at the wells of tradition is an important part of our task as parents and educators.

In the Old Testament we see the importance of faith as a tradition, a heritage passed down from generation to generation. In the sixth chapter of the book of Deuteronomy when Moses was given commandments for the people of God, parents were instructed to teach these commandments to their children and to pass them on to subsequent generations. And not only the commandments themselves were to be taught, but the very history of God's dealings with His people.

There is a false perception that Jesus completely condemned tradition. Some people will point to passages like Mark 7:8,9 or Matthew 15:3 to demonstrate the supposed negative attitude that Jesus held toward tradition. But a careful reading of these passages will clarify that it is not tradition itself that He condemned, only false and shallow tradition. Jesus condemned the kind of tradition that exalts itself above the commands of God and replaces religion of the heart with empty and lifeless formulas. This kind of tradition rests safely in the past without due appreciation for what God is doing in the present or will do in the future. It is a tradition that idolizes the past but does not see that the past is valuable to us primarily because it teaches us how to live in the present.

Many fail to comprehend the difference between tradition and traditionalism. Jaroslav Pelikan differentiates cogently between the two: Tradition is "the living faith of the dead," which can still affect us in positive ways, nurturing and challenging us, and traditionalism is "the dead faith of the living," which holds onto the outward rituals and rhetoric of belief but does not burn with an inner fire of passion for God.

Ultimately, tradition in the church is the ongoing, living influence of the Holy Spirit. Because God is alive and His Spirit is alive, the truth renews itself on a continual basis. The truth is ever fresh. But at the same time the truth is ever the same; it does not change. We do not look for new truth, but for the truth to constantly make itself heard anew. Simone Weil wrote that "to be always relevant, you have to say things which are eternal."

Tradition tells us that we need to be attentive to the past and to what we can learn from it. According to G. K. Chesterton, tradition is the important task of learning from the wisdom of those who have gone before us:

> Tradition may be defined as an extension of the franchise. Tradition means giving votes to the most obscure of all classes, our ancestors. It is the democracy of the dead. Tradition refuses to submit to the small and arrogant oligarchy of those who merely happen to be walking about.[1]

Some will argue, of course, that we do not need to listen to the voice of the past, but only need to hear God in the present. Such a negative attitude toward tradition may be at its root a spiritual problem. It could indicate an overwhelming and arrogant pride in ourselves and our own resources. I can remember as a young Christian being counseled against reading Bible commentaries and works of theology because, I was told, all I really needed was the Bible itself. If I were to read only the Bible, then all that I needed to know could be drawn from its pages. This idea troubled me for some time until I realized the hidden arrogance of believing that I did not need the insights and revelations of those who had preceded me. To suggest that I would be harmed by the insights of brilliant and godly men and women of the past and present is a folly that is truly dangerous. Are we not the body of Christ? Is not the body of Christ extended over time as well as space? Do we not need each other? Are our ancestors in the faith not of any importance to us today?

The philosopher Leo Strauss has pointed out that in any one generation there are only a handful of truly great minds who will be contemporary with us. This means that if our minds are to be instructed by the most insightful of human minds, this learning must take place primarily through the instrument of books. In great books we encounter great minds.

Indeed, all of our present achievements and insights are based upon ideas and discoveries which preceded them. We progress by listening to the past, by asking questions of it, sometimes by arguing with it. In his seminal essay *Tradition and Individual Talent,* T. S. Eliot has expressed well the concept of the correct use of the past:

If the only form of tradition, of handing down, con-
sisted in following the ways of the immediate generation before us in a blind or timid adherence to its
successes, "tradition" should positively be discour-
aged. We have seen many such simple currents soon
lost in the sand; and novelty is better than repetition.
Tradition is a matter of much wider significance. It
cannot be inherited, and if you want it you must
obtain it by great labor.[2]

As Eliot points out so well, tradition is not the same as
conformity. In considering the importance of tradition, we are
not talking about a thoughtless following of past ways and
ideas. Instead, what we must understand is that our contemporary work is part of a succession from the past, and that we
function best in the present when we take the past into
account. We do not need to reinvent the wheel in each generation. Can you imagine how slowly science would progress if
each and every scientist had to go back to the beginning and
rediscover the basic laws of science for himself? Instead, sci-
entists build on the work of those who have gone before
them, as we do in every area of our lives every day.

Bernardus of Silvestris, a twelfth-century monk, wrote
regarding the successes of his own day: "We see farther
because we stand on the shoulders of giants." So it is for us.
As believers we stand on the shoulders of the likes of
Augustine, Aquinas, Luther, Calvin, and Jonathan Edwards.
We can build on their insights and use their perspectives as a
vantage point to critique our own time. Sometimes it is difficult to see our own cultural attitudes and ideas clearly and
objectively because they are so much a part of us. Like the air

around us, we cannot see them clearly because we are surrounded by them and they tend to become invisible to us. But from the vantage point of a former time and place, gained through attentive reading of the classics of our tradition, we can see how time-bound and ungodly some of our own cherished prejudices really are. "Someone has said: 'The dead writers are remote from us because we know so much more than they did.' Precisely," writes T. S. Eliot, "and they are that which we know." [3]

An attitude that is widespread in our culture is that our present time is so progressive that we no longer have need of our "barbaric" past. The fact that we are progressing is easy to see in the realm of technology and machinery. I have seen, in my own lifetime, rapid changes and transformations in all kinds of technology. What was once only dreamed of is now almost humdrum. Unfortunately, the concept of a constant progress which leaves the past behind has carried over into the realm of human thought and culture. That which is more recent is conceived of as more enlightened than what preceded it. C. S. Lewis labels this kind of thinking "chronological snobbery." Lewis writes in his autobiography about how his friend Owen Barfield questioned his youthful trust in the merely contemporary, and how he was cured of this attitude:

> Barfield . . . made short work of what I have called
> my "chronological snobbery," the uncritical accep-
> tance of the intellectual climate common to our age
> and the assumption that whatever has gone out of
> date is on that account discredited. You must find out
> why it went out of date; was it ever refuted (and if so

by whom, where and how conclusively) or did it merely die away as fashions do? If the latter, this tells us nothing about its truth or falsehood. From seeing this one passes to the realization that our age is also a "period," and certainly has, like all periods, its own characteristic illusions. They are likeliest to lurk in those widespread assumptions which are so ingrained in the age that no one dares to attack or feels it necessary to defend them.[4]

Lewis believed that the myth of progress was a powerfully motivating force in modern society. In an essay called "The Funeral of a Great Myth," Lewis draws a distinction between the scientific theory of evolution and the popular idea of evolution as progressive improvement in all areas of existence. The result of this myth of constant progress is to cause us to place great (and unwarranted) trust in our present understandings. Instead of looking to Aristotle or Aquinas for a moral theory, we concentrate on the latest prognostications of the social-science pundits. We treat the thinking of the past as irrelevant, thereby cutting ourselves off from its riches. Being cut off from tradition, we rob ourselves of a source that would provide us with a standpoint from which we can critique our own age.

Above all, tradition frees us from the siren song of relevancy. All the voices around us seem to be crying out the importance of making education "relevant." Unfortunately, what this usually means is making ourselves slaves of the contemporary, following the pied piper of the latest trend or fad. We use our perceived freedom from the constraints of the past to follow blindly the whims of the moment. We are busily trying to catch the next wave of innovation. But as Dean Inge wrote, "He who is married to the spirit of the age will soon find himself a widower." While the "relevant" is ever shifting and changing, the truths embedded in tradition remain constant.

Tradition is also a fountainhead of creativity. Paradoxically, the work of artists and thinkers who immersed themselves most in the traditions of the past are among the most creative. Pablo Picasso, T. S. Eliot, and James Joyce all made striking innovations in their fields. All of them were patient students of the traditions out of which their art arose.

The past is a priceless treasure. We need to recapture a sense of our place in the unfolding of God's plan for the ages and an appreciation for the "communion of saints"—the contribution of believers throughout time. Thomas Oden, a theologian who spent much of his early theological career focused on the latest cultural and theological whims, has increasingly become committed to the importance of the writings of the early church. "Once hesitant to trust anyone over thirty," he writes, "now I hesitate to trust anyone under three hundred." Oden bemoans the lack of historical perspective he sees in the modern church:

> [We] need to recover a sense of the active work of the Spirit in history, through living communities. Our modern individualism too easily tempts us to take our Bible and remove ourselves from the wider believing community. We end up with a Bible and a radio, but no church.[5]

And so I put forth the challenge to reacquaint yourselves with the riches of the Christian tradition. Read the great books of the Christian tradition, study them in groups, pass them around in churches, teach their ideas to your children. You will find that sometimes you can gain a new perspective from the refreshingly old.

2

Why Read the Christian Classics?

*The man who doesn't read good books has no
advantage over the man who can't read them.*

—MARK TWAIN

*When you reread a classic you do not see more in
the book than you did before; you see more in you than
was there before.*

—CLIFTON FADIMAN

*It is chiefly through books that we enjoy intercourse
with superior minds. . . . In the best books, great men
talk to us, give us their most precious thoughts, and
pour their souls into ours.*

WILLIAM ELLERY CHANNING

In the church today there is an abysmal lack of awareness of both the historical rootedness and the creative richness of our faith. Reading the Christian classics is one of the surest ways to broaden and deepen our faith and our commitment. There are a number of positive results that will arise from time spent with these great books.

Appreciating Our Diversity

Reading the great Christian books helps us to appreciate the diversity within the body of Christ, both currently and over time. Our differences may be real, but as we grow in an awareness of the variety of ideas and possible expressions of them within the Christian tradition, it may help us to see how few people there are in history who agree with us exactly on every point. This helps to relativize our own sense of always being in the right and causes us to focus on what C. S. Lewis called "mere Christianity"—the handful of essential ideas that distinguish Christianity from other faiths and ideologies. We will see several common themes which run throughout the great Christian writings and realize how much we can learn even from those with whom we have violent disagreements. For example, while

Calvinists and Arminians may never fully agree about providence, free will, and human freedom, Calvinists can learn to appreciate the penetrating insights of John Wesley; and Arminians, the rich thought of John Calvin. In so doing, we might also find ourselves striking new positions of balance and tolerance. We can also much more clearly understand our own positions when we see them set up against the positions of others as articulated by our "adversaries" themselves.

Appreciating the Depth of Our Heritage

A wide reading in these great books demonstrates the depth and profundity of our tradition. Many accuse orthodox Christianity of being anticultural. A tradition which can boast of the likes of Bach, Dostoevski, Rembrandt, Kierkegaard, Rouault, Flannery O'Connor, Donne, Handel, Dante and Pascal cannot fairly be dismissed as narrow, sterile and lacking in creative thrust. As the contemporary songwriter/performer T-Bone Burnett has written:

> I was asked, "Do you think Christianity is a fad?"
> "A fad," I wondered.
> And I thought about C. S. Lewis and G. K. Chesterton
> And T. S. Eliot.
> And I thought about Tolstoy and Dostoevski.
> And Reubens and van Gogh and Rembrandt.
> And Handel and Haydn and Bach.
> And Luther.
> And Pascal.
> And Dante Alighieri.

And à Kempis and Augustine.
And Paul of Tarsis and Simon Peter.
"It's been going on for years," I thought.
"Back to about one."

In a world whose memory
Goes back to about 1963,
A world cut off from the past,
It is important to discover our history.
Because we are all leaves on a tree.[1]

We do indeed have a heritage in which we can take pride. Some of the finest artistic and creative achievements of all time were born out of the Christian gospel.

Asking the Perennial Questions

Reading the great books can help us to understand how perennial the great questions of our faith are. Who is God? What is His role in human existence? What is mankind? What is our essential nature? What does the future hold? These books provide ever-new insights into these great questions. We can read them again and again, as they always seem to have something new to say to us, providing resources for the continued discussion of these issues. And because these works often disagree with one another, we learn to read dialectically, with an open and questioning mind.

Our lives are so busy, assailed with what must be done this moment, that we often are consumed with the immediate, urgent needs and distracted from the solitude in which the questions of life can be contemplated. It is a sad truth that the most important questions of life are the first thing to go when life becomes harried. At the time we most need the truths found in the great questions, we tell ourselves that we don't have time to think on such things. If we do not ask these questions, we do not grow and learn. The great books confront us with important issues which demand a response.

Seeing Beyond Today

Reading in the classics will also give us a perspective that is broader than the merely contemporary. In modern Christendom we are often prone to faddishness, placing our concerns in the ephemeral and transient rather than the weighty and eternal. We get caught up in debating issues like the interpretation of biblical prophecy, attempting to discern the signs of the last days and to "pin the tail on the Antichrist." Over ten years' experience working in a Christian bookstore has given me perspective on how theological fads come and go with alarming rapidity. Yesterday's burning issue becomes forgotten tomorrow as we dizzily chase the latest trends. A proper grounding in the great traditions of the church would help keep us on an even keel, making us properly skeptical of the "latest thinking" and keeping us focused on the critical essentials of the Christian faith.

Building a Christian Vision

These works are also valuable in that they can help us to understand that Christianity is not just an abstract set of beliefs, but rather a vision of reality. Sometimes we can get so wrapped up in the doctrinal assertions of faith that we lose touch with the fact that the Christian faith is a comprehensive way of viewing the world, what Edith Schaeffer called "a way of seeing." It is particularly the works of fine art, poetry, and fiction which are such a rich part of our heritage in providing us with a creative vision for the world and our place within it. They demonstrate that the Christian will see his or her world in a different light from the nonbeliever. And this vision, as a sampling of these fine classic works will demonstrate, is marked by a realism about human limitations, coupled with profound hope and glorious promise. Learning to communicate this aesthetic vision will make us more effective in our presentation of the gospel, as people are more deeply moved by a compelling vision of reality than they are by intellectual argument.

Learning from the Past

Finally, the classics teach us about the mistakes and triumphs of those who have gone before us. These great books are not to be thought of as infallible sources of wisdom. They are, indeed, a record of much wisdom and insight. But they are also a record of false starts, wrong conclusions, human frailty, and stubbornness. Like us, these writers are fallen individuals whose own preconceptions and self-deceptions creep in. But even these mistakes can help us to see more clearly. Sometimes we can only fully discern the truth in juxtaposition with error. It is so easy to catch ourselves buying into ideas that represent what we *want* to believe to be true, rather than accepting the sometimes uncomfortable truth.

C. S. Lewis offered sage advice when he wrote, "It is a good rule, after reading a new book, never to allow yourself another new one till you have read an old one in between." I offer the following list of "Great Books of the Christian Tradition" to help you begin or continue your own exploration of the valuable resources of our Christian heritage.

3

The Great Books of the Christian Tradition

If he shall not lose his reward who gives a cup of cold water to his thirsty neighbor, what will not be the reward of those who by putting books into the hands of those neighbors, open to them the fountains of eternal life?

—THOMAS À KEMPIS

You can find all the new ideas in the old books; only there you will find them balanced, kept in their place, and sometimes contradicted and overcome by other and better ideas. The great writers did not neglect a fad because they had not thought of it, but because they had thought of it and of all the answers to it as well.

—G.K. CHESTERTON

Let us thank God for books. When I consider what some books have done for the world, and what they are doing, how they keep up our hope, awaken new courage and faith, soothe pain, give an ideal life to those whose homes are cold and hard, bind together distant ages and foreign lands, create new worlds of beauty, bringing down truths from heaven—I give eternal blessings for this gift, and pray that we may use it aright, and abuse it not.

—JAMES FREEMAN CLARKE

A Brief Word
About This List

The list that follows is the result of many years' invest-
ment of time in reading, researching, comparing the
lists of others, adding, and deleting. Although it began as a
project to guide my own personal reading, other people have
found it helpful for themselves. I made the list available to
some friends who wanted to see it and then to others who
asked for a copy. I finally decided to make it public, with
some revision and expanded annotations. I do not offer it as
a definitive statement. In many ways, it is a work in progress
and probably, by its very nature, always will be. I see it as a
starting point, not as a terminus.

For all its imperfections, however, I am convinced that it
is a useful guide to those who want to make the best use of
their reading time. There are a myriad of choices out there
when it comes to books. Most of what is published each year
is of little value for anything more than whiling away idle
hours, or providing a little entertainment. But great books
expose us to great minds and spirits, and being in the

presence of greatness cannot but change us. This is a list of books that have proven themselves to be great. Some readers will undoubtedly take issue with certain things included or left out; but there is, I think, nothing of indisputable importance that is missing. Reading these books will provide a good introduction to the fundamental ideas and important persons in our tradition of faith.

One of the false ideas about developing a canon (or definitive list) of important books is that, once chosen, the list is written in stone. This is far from the case. Over time, books once ignored are recognized to be of great value, and those once thought truly great are seen to be more transitory and ephemeral. The canon of great books is (and should be) self-adjusting over time. In recent decades we have seen the need to take a second look at the work of women and minorities and to reevaluate their contribution—a contribution once sadly ignored. Over time, therefore, the list of great books will change and develop. I would welcome suggestions on how this list might be improved.

I hope it will be obvious that I do not personally agree with everything in every book on this list. If I did, I would hold a widely contradictory set of beliefs, even if I limited myself to the books in the Christian tradition. For these authors share in a dialogue which has occurred over the ages concerning the nature of God and man, the purpose of human life, and the methods and beliefs which further that purpose.

This "great conversation," as Mortimer Adler and Robert Hutchins have referred to it, consists of the continuing process of give-and-take which results in deeper understandings. On this side of eternity, there is much that we do not and cannot know. This dialogue, these arguments, this conversation help us to draw closer to the truth. I offer this list not to buttress my own convictions, but to introduce the reader to the important questions of life and to how great minds have struggled with them. I personally disagree with much of what some of the authors state. In some cases, the authors on this list are polar opposites of one another on key issues. In other cases, whether they properly belong in the Christian tradition at all is perhaps a matter for debate. I simply let the authors speak for themselves. If they have called themselves a Christian, however heterodox at times, I have included them. Your own definitions of Christianity may not be so charitable. That is okay. Just remember that even the heretics may have much to teach us, or may at least cause us to look more closely at the questions of life. Liberal and conservative, Protestant, Catholic, and Eastern Orthodox, therefore, all stand in the list together.

You will notice that the list gets longer as we arrive at periods nearer to our own time. This is emphatically not because there are more significant books written now than in the past. Rather, it is because we do not have the benefit of time to help us distinguish those books which are truly important and influential from those that only seem to be. No one, I think, will argue with the statement that Augustine is a vitally important writer—he is considered so by any standard. But who from the twentieth century will still be read and quoted a thousand years from now . . . or even a hundred? Though we cannot know, I have provided the names of some writers whose merit seems, in my opinion, high enough (for various reasons) to be at least candidates for literary immortality. Also, because the point of the list is to help us continue the ongoing dialogue of the church throughout the ages, the very recent voices are ones we must contend with, for their words still hang in the cultural air around us.

Finally, believing that all truth is God's truth, wherever it is found—in the mouth of sinner or saint; and that we need to understand the sources of even those ideas we disagree with, I offer in chapter 5 a second list: those books which have shaped and formed our modern consciousness. I do this in the belief that it is better to argue against the best statement of an untruth than a clumsily stated and carica-tured one. Let us not battle straw men, but seek what it is that poisons the stream at its headwaters. Let us criticize, for example, Marx or Freud or Darwin on the basis of what they really said, not on the basis of inaccurate hearsay. We owe at least that much to the cause of truth.

The Ancient World

*I*n the first centuries after Christ, the church faced the challenge of developing a systematic presentation of the Christian gospel. Challenged by many diverse heresies, and sometimes threatened by martyrdom, Christians faced the challenge of explaining the content of the gospel and its implications for daily life to a culture filled with competing religious systems. They left us a heritage of courageous proclamation and the wisdom that comes from close study of Scripture and prayerful surrender to God. Though their names are unfamiliar to many modern Christians, we owe a great debt to these early believers.

◆ ◆ ◆

The Bible

In earlier times, it might have gone without saying that the Bible is the key book for understanding the mysteries of human nature and the reality of a sphere of existence beyond the purely material realm. Even to those for whom the Bible is merely a historical oddity, it must be admitted that it has had a profound influence on the way that people in the West view themselves and their world. The great literature of our culture is littered with references and allusions to the Bible. As one great critic put it, you cannot understand most of the great literature of our civilization if you are not familiar with the Bible and with Shakespeare. The Bible's thoughts, ideas, personalities, and phrases are the coin in which much of our conversation is transacted.

To the eyes of faith, however, the Bible is much more: an inexhaustible source of wisdom and insight into the very mind of God. It is the Word of God. As St. Jerome wrote, "Ignorance of the Scriptures is ignorance of Christ." The Bible is the foundation for theology, a guide for the spiritual life, a foundation for ethics, and a testimony to the power and grace of God in human history. The Bible should be read devotionally, studied intensely, and its teachings practiced faithfully.

There are many good modern translations. For accuracy I would recommend the New International Version, the New American Standard Version, or the New Revised Standard Version. For beauty there is no comparison to the rich poetic cadences of the King James Version.

The Apostolic Fathers

Selected Writings

The writings of the Apostolic Fathers give us a look at the church in its infancy. Many readers will be surprised to find how institutionalized the church was even in these early days, and how similar some of the issues they dealt with are to those which are still with us. Among the writings of this group of early church leaders are:

The Didache (author unknown; probably written in the middle of the second century) is a manual of church order and Christian ethics. It gives a fascinating look at the practice and the liturgy of the early church.

Both Clement (*Letter to the Corinthians,* c. 96) and Ignatius (various letters, c. 107) dwelt primarily on two issues: the necessity for loyalty to the bishops as God-ordained authority, and the importance of avoiding doctrinal entrapment by the heretics who were abundant in those times.

Justin Martyr (100–165) was the first Christian apologist, one who argued the truth of Christianity against its pagan opponents. Unashamed, he argued against the intellectual elite of his day that Christianity was the most rational of faiths. His fearless defense of the gospel eventually brought him the crown of a martyr when he refused to worship the state gods of Rome.

The Shepherd of Hermas (c. 130) is an account of revelations made to Hermas by the church, which appears in the form of a woman; a shepherd who represents repentance; and a great angel. This book, very popular in the early church, is an allegory of sin, repentance, and baptism.

Irenaeus (d. 202) also died a martyr. He is credited with being the first real theologian of the early church. In his works his powerful, logical mind is exercised in spelling out the key doctrines of the faith.

Tertullian (c. 160–220) was one of the greatest of the Christian apologists. Though best known for his statement, "I believe because it is absurd," he worked hard to show that Christianity should be accepted by the Roman empire because the ethics and lifestyle of believers make them among the best of citizens.

The classic English translation of the Apostolic Fathers is that of Lightfoot. If you can locate a copy of the lively modern translation (with introductions and notes) by Jack Sparks, it will help to make the reading much easier.

Athanasius (c. 296–373)

On the Incarnation
Life of St. Antony

Athanasius has been long regarded as one of the most important and saintly theological thinkers of the early church. His contemporaries said of him that "he is a sincere, virtuous man, a good Christian, an ascetic, a true bishop." His key role in the Council of Nicaea helped guard the church against the heresies that were so powerful in his time.

On the Incarnation is one of the keys works of the early church. In it, Athanasius attempts to give a rational explanation for the key Christian doctrine (the incarnation of God in Jesus Christ) and to elaborate on its meaning for the lives of believers. I would especially recommend the edition published by SVS Press which includes a marvelous preface by C. S. Lewis, and a brief commentary on the Psalms by Athanasius containing powerful spiritual insights on this important biblical book.

While *On the Incarnation* shows the theological acumen of Athanasius, the *Life of St. Antony* gives a glimpse of his spiritual insight as he writes one of the earliest spiritual biographies of the founder of the monastic way. This book teaches that the central occupation of the Christian life is the struggle to bring the flesh under control. Athanasius knew Antony personally and embraced the ascetic form of spirituality that Antony practiced, believing that only a life lived in holiness would open the heart to God.

———————————————— ♦♦♦ ————————————————

You know how it is when some great king enters a large city and dwells in one of its houses; because of his dwelling in that single house, the whole city is honoured, and enemies and robbers cease to molest it. Even so is it with the King of all; He has come into our country and dwelt in one body amidst the many, and in consequence the designs of the enemy against mankind have been foiled, and the corruption of death, which formerly held them in its power, has simply ceased to be. For the human race would have perished utterly had not the Lord and Saviour of all, the Son of God, come among us to put an end to death.

—St. Athanasius, *On the Incarnation*

❖❖❖

The Desert Fathers

Selections

The Desert Fathers were forerunners of monasticism who left their lives in the cities and countryside to live as hermits or in small communities in the desert. The writings of the Desert Fathers consist of miracle stories, feats of incredible asceticism and, most importantly, penetrating insight into human nature. By leaving "the world" and looking inside themselves, they made many powerful discoveries.

The intriguing and often eccentric writings of these forerunners of the monastic tradition are filled with numerous examples of sly wisdom, negation of the self, and absolute surrender to God. At times these writings are merely strange and sometimes a bit repulsive, but more often they burn white-hot with revelation about human limitations and the necessity of complete dedication to God. Thomas Merton has edited a lively collection of their writings under the title *The Wisdom of the Desert*. You may also find a helpful introduction to the spiritual riches of the Desert Fathers in Henri Nouwen's superb little book *The Way of the Heart*.

Eusebius (c. 260–339)

Ecclesiastical History

Eusebius is often called "the father of church history"—a title he earned by his extensive history of the Christian church during its first three centuries. Written in ten books over a period of 15 years, it has stood the test of time. Most church historians agree that it is substantially accurate. Were it not for Eusebius, much of the history of the early church would remain largely unknown to us.

Augustine (345–430)

Confessions
The City of God

Augustine's *Confessions* is quite simply one of the greatest books ever written. It repays frequent rereading. Each time I read it, I am impressed with new insights that I am surprised I did not discover on earlier readings. This searchingly honest autobiographical account of a soul in search of God will undoubtedly provoke soul-searching on the part of the reader. It tells the story of Augustine's intellectual and spiritual journey through several major philosophies of his day, and of his awakening to the fact that only God could bring him freedom from the struggle with his flesh. Arguably the first real autobiography in Western culture, *Confessions* is written in the form of prayers of thanksgiving and praise to God. The exquisite beauty of Augustine's prose is well-captured in the translation by R. S. Pine-Coffin or that of Fulton Sheen.

The City of God is a much longer, more philosophical and historical book, and of much less interest to the casual reader, but it is an unquestionably important document in the development of a Christian view of history and culture. For those not prepared to tackle this very long book, it is still worth skimming. Augustine's doctrinal study, *On the Trinity*, is also recommended.

Peter Brown's *Augustine of Hippo* is an outstanding biography of Augustine which illuminates his many contributions to the Western intellectual and spiritual tradition.

———————————— ◆◆◆ ————————————

I have learned to love you late, Beauty at once so ancient and so new! I have learned to love you late! You were within me, and I was in the world outside myself. I searched for you outside myself and, disfigured as I was, I fell upon the lovely things of your creation. You were with me, but I was not with you. The beautiful things of this world kept me far from you and yet, if they had not been in you, they would have had no being at all. You called me; you cried aloud to me; you broke my barrier of deafness. You shone upon me; your radiance enveloped me; you put my blindness to flight. You shed your fragrance about me; I drew breath and now I gasp for your sweet odor. I tasted you, and now I hunger and thirst for you. You touched me, and I am inflamed with love of your peace.

—Augustine, *The Confessions*

———————————— ◆◆◆ ————————————

John Chrysostom (c. 347–407)

Sermons

Chrysostom, whose name means "golden mouth," was certainly that. In his day, he was known for his skill in preaching from the Scriptures in a way that was practical, beautiful, imaginative, and intellectually compelling. In a time when the allegorical method was the most common way of approaching the Bible, Chrysostom urged a literal interpretation whenever possible. Because of this approach, his expository sermons on Genesis, Matthew, John, and the Pauline epistles are still valuable and insightful today.

Benedict (c. 480–c. 543)

The Rule of St. Benedict

Benedict's rule can be credited with bringing a stabilizing influence to the monastic life. His rule is a short and insightful guide to the monastic life by the man who turned it into an organized system. Benedict built his view of the monastic life (a view that still prevails today) around three emphases: obedience to the hierarchy within the monastery, regular prayer, and manual labor. What is still so striking about this rule is its balance. While it contains enough strictness to restrain the excesses of the flesh, it is also realistic enough about human nature not to be discouraging or overwhelmingly impossible to live by.

The Middle Ages

*T*he very term "middle ages" is an indication of the way many people view this time period. For some, this period was simply the gap between the ancient and modern periods, a time of intellectual stagnation and mindless following of tradition. But such a characterization is not entirely fair, for while this may not have been a time of striking scientific innovation, it was certainly a time of great fertility in the Christian tradition. Though authority played its role as a steadying influence, much original and creative thinking and writing was taking place.

◆◆◆

Anselm of Canterbury (c. 1033–1109)

Monologium

Proslogium

These two important works of theology are concerned with building a logical case for the existence of God. Anselm's most notable achievement is the ontological proof for the existence of God. In brief, the ontological argument states that the fact that we are able to entertain the idea of God ("that than which nothing greater can be conceived") requires that God actually exist. In other words, if God did not objectively exist, we wouldn't even be able to imagine such a being. Whether or not you find this argument persuasive, in the oversimplified form I have expressed it, it has been much debated and defended by theologians down through the years. One of the interesting characteristics of these two works is that they are written in the form of a series of prayers. The idea that theology can and should be done in the midst of prayer is certainly an appealing one.

Bernard of Clairvaux (1090–1153)

On the Love of God
Sermons on the Song of Songs

Though Bernard was a very important man of his time, heavily involved in the religious and political struggles of his day, his writings reveal that he was also a man deeply in love with God. *On the Love of God* emphasizes God as the very basis and ground of love in all its forms. Bernard's sermons on the Song of Songs (better known today as the Song of Solomon) are an allegorical and mystical interpretation of this passionate biblical book. Jesus Himself is the Bridegroom, and we are the Bride and recipients of His overwhelming love. This is beautiful writing on God's passionate love for us, and an expression of deep personal devotion to the Savior.

A refreshingly sensual experience of God written in a time characterized by a dry scholasticism.

Peter Abelard (1079–1142)

Letters of Abelard and Heloise

Abelard was one of the most famous and respected theological teachers of the Middle Ages. This collection of letters recounts his illicit romance with a young girl he was tutoring, which resulted in his castration (by order of the girl's angry father) and her forced exile to a convent.

Their tragic tale of temptation and guilt is honest and self-searching. While it reads with all the excitement of a modern novel, there is much profound reflection in these pages on human sin, the lure of illicit sexuality, and a demonstration of forgiveness and the need for change.

Francis of Assisi (1181–1226)

Little Flowers of St. Francis

The joyful tales about Francis and his followers are filled with wonder, sacrifice, and devotion. These delightful and miraculous tales expound the exploits of Francis and his band of followers. The reader is overwhelmed by Francis's childlike trust and simplicity of heart, and by his resulting spiritual power. One quickly senses why he was one of the great spiritual leaders of all time and why the devotion to his simple message still lives on. Francis was perhaps the most Christlike man who ever lived. Read G. K. Chesterton's book *St. Francis* for a loving but unsentimental retelling of his life.

— ◆ ◆ ◆ —

Lord, make me an instrument of Thy peace;
  where there is hatred, let me sow love;
  where there is injury, pardon;
  where there is doubt, faith;
  where there is despair, hope;
  where there is darkness, light;
  and where there is sadness, joy.
O Divine Master,
  grant that I may not so much seek
  to be consoled as to console;
  to be understood as to understand;
  to be loved as to love;
  for it is in giving that we receive,
  it is in pardoning that we are pardoned,
  and it is in dying that we are born to eternal life.
                                        —Francis of Assisi

— ◆ ◆ ◆ —

Thomas Aquinas (c. 1225–1274)

Summa Theologica

Aquinas was one of the most profound and prolific thinkers of all time. During his life he covered enough pages with words to fill over 100 volumes. His masterwork was the *Summa Theologica,* a massive work of theology which itself fills a number of volumes. Aquinas's lifelong goal was to wed faith and reason together. He taught that the Christian faith is not inherently opposed to the life of the mind, and he worked hard to show that faith can be defended, and its opponents rebutted, by reason. In reading his work, one is struck by its careful logic, its fairness to those he disagrees with, and its deep loyalty to Scripture and church tradition. This book is the benchmark of Catholic theology.

If you don't want to try to tackle the whole thing (it is certainly intimidating in its length!), the condensation with notes by Peter Kreeft entitled *Summa of the Summa* is an excellent place to begin.

Dante Aligheri (1265–1321)

La Vita Nuova
The Divine Comedy

Dante's masterpiece is the story of a mythical journey through hell, purgatory, and paradise. The attentive reader absorbs theological learning, political satire, and engaging drama in one of the greatest books of all time. The writing is beautiful, and Dante is passionate about what he believes. While a book for the ages, it is also a book rooted in its time. Dante is unsparing in his criticism of corruption and unrighteousness, especially as seen in the church hierarchy. In fact, he denounced most of the contemporary popes, placing them in his fictionalized hell.

I highly recommend the very fine annotated translation by John Ciardi. Also worth noting is the vivid translation by Dorothy L. Sayers.

Dante's earlier work, *La Vita Nuova* (*The New Life*), is a poetic meditation on the nature of romantic love and its relationship to divine love. It introduces us to the beautiful Beatrice, who plays the role of his guide through heaven in *The Divine Comedy.* Here, his love for her awakens within him a love for God.

——————————————— ◆◆◆ ———————————————

Midway in our life's journey, I went astray
    from the straight road and woke to find myself
    alone in a dark wood. How shall I say
what wood that was! I never saw so drear,
    so rank, so arduous a wilderness!
    Its very memory gives a shape to fear.
Death could scarce be more bitter than that place!
    But since it came to good I will recount
    all that I found revealed there by God's grace.

—Dante Aligheri, *Inferno*

——————————————— ◆◆◆ ———————————————

Author Unknown

The Cloud of Unknowing

This important mystical treatise is on the incomprehensibility of God and our inability to capture an understanding of

God through the limited resources of our human conceptions. God, says the anonymous author, dwells beyond all our concepts in a divine "dazzling darkness." Many will feel the author goes too far at points, but he is a healthy corrective to the cocksure theology that claims to fully comprehend the person and plan of God. A little mystery can be a very healthy thing.

Richard Rolle (c. 1300–1349)

The Fire of Love

Rolle left Oxford University at age 19 to become a hermit. His experience of God's presence as a rapturous and life-transforming warmth in his heart changed his life forever. In lyrical and often alliterative prose, Rolle celebrates the intoxicating love of God. He emphasizes that God can best be known not through the efforts of the human mind, but through a heart that is touched by the Savior. The translation by M. L. del Mastro captures the beauty of Rolle's prose style.

Juliana of Norwich (1343–1413)

Revelations of Divine Love

Through the revelations that Juliana was given by God, she reflects meditatively on the nurturing, "feminine" side of God and upon the all-encompassing love and mercy of God. Please do not mistake her meditations on God's mothering actions in our lives with the feminist or goddess theology which has become so prevalent in recent years. What Juliana is pointing to is God's role as both mother and father in the lives of believers. Writing at a time when the sternness and unapproachability of God were emphasized, Juliana brings balance with this vision of God's incomprehensible love, grace, and mercy. When we know Him in whom we place our trust, as Juliana writes, "All shall be well and all shall be well and all manner of things shall be well."

—————————————— ♦♦♦ ——————————————

And in this He [God] showed me something small, not bigger than a hazelnut, lying in the palm of my hand, as it seemed to me, and it was round as a ball. I looked at it with the eye of my understanding and thought: What can this be? I was amazed that it could last for I thought that because of its littleness, it would surely have fallen into nothing. And I was answered in my understanding: It lasts, and always will, because God loves it; and thus everything has being through the love of God.

—Juliana of Norwich, *Revelations of Divine Love*

—————————————— ♦♦♦ ——————————————

Geoffrey Chaucer (c. 1343–1400)

The Canterbury Tales

This collection of tales, sometimes profound, sometimes bawdy, ranges over all aspects of human existence. Chaucer gives us a collection of stories told by a group of pilgrims to while away the passing miles on their way to the church at Canterbury. The stories are by turns amusing, moving, heroic, tragic, sensual, and inspirational. Here is truly "all God's plenty" in His human creation: the good, the bad, the honest, the despicable, and the holy. A marvelous cornucopia of stories.

Those who question the faith of Chaucer (whom some modern critics have suggested was an agnostic) should look again at his epilogue, where he dedicates both the work and his life to God. The original Old English text is recommended only for the diligent and adventurous. For most people, a modern translation will make the book more enjoyable.

Catherine of Sienna (1347–1380)

The Spiritual Dialogue

One of the most striking things about Catherine of Sienna was her balance of the active and the contemplative life. From her youngest days, she had a deeply experiential relationship with God and would find herself lost in mystical rapture. By the age of 20, however, she had dedicated her life to caring for the sick, especially those suffering from diseases that most people found revolting. Although a mystic, her life of contemplation was balanced by a life of sacrificial service. Her holiness was so obvious that rulers of both church and state came to her for advice and spiritual guidance.

Her book *The Spiritual Dialogue* describes the pathway to holiness for the believer, emphasizing the "Precious Blood of Christ" as the surest evidence of God's love for us. The balance of her life is evident in her writings as she emphasizes that God primarily uses normal and ordinary people as the channels of His love and grace.

Thomas à Kempis (c. 1380–1471)

On the Imitation of Christ

One of the bestselling books of all time, this devotional classic is marked by its call for single-minded devotion to

Jesus Christ and a simple, uncluttered life of adoration. Thomas à Kempis calls us to imitate Christ's life and to practice His teachings with humility and trust in the grace of God. Within these pages are some of the most heart-stirring and convicting passages in all of devotional literature. One of the most sane and balanced of all the mystics, à Kempis through this book has been deeply influential in the lives of countless believers.

Do not try to read the book too quickly or digest too much of it at one time. Some people have found it repetitive, but that is part of its art. Read in small doses, you will find à Kempis returning again and again to his main themes. The cumulative force is challenging and transforming. It is a book to be savored, prayed over, and meditated upon.

◆ ◆ ◆

What good can it do you to discuss the mystery of God in the Trinity in learned terms if you lack humility and so displease that God? Learned arguments do not make a man holy and righteous, whereas a good life makes him dear to God. I would rather feel compunction in my heart than be able to define it. If you knew the whole Bible off by heart and all the expositions of scholars, what good would it do you without the love and grace of God?

—Thomas à Kempis, *On the Imitation of Christ*

◆ ◆ ◆

The Early Modern World

*T*he Reformation was the key event of this period in the Christian tradition. The era we know as the Renaissance was characterized by a freedom of intellectual inquiry and a growing sense of individualism, the belief that each person is unique and important. In the area of religious faith this produced a willingness to question the traditional church authority, a renewed search for the individual experience of God's grace, and a desire to probe deeply into the hard realities of the human condition. Out of this period came some of the most profound works of western history in theology, philosophy, and literature.

♦ ♦ ♦

Martin Luther (1483–1546)

The Freedom of the Christian
Bondage of the Will
Table Talk

The great Reformer writes powerfully of salvation by faith alone and the power of grace. His theological works are seminal for understanding the history of theology, and his *Table Talk* reveals something of Luther the man: his brilliance, devotion, and sense of humor.

Two of the better recent biographies are those of Roland Bainton *(Here I Stand)* and Heiko Oberman *(Luther: Man Between God and the Devil)*.

— ◆ ◆ ◆ —

Nothing makes a man good except faith, nor evil except unbelief.

It is indeed true that in the sight of men a man is made good or evil by his works, but this being made good or evil is no more than that he who is good or evil is pointed out and known as such. . . . He, therefore, who does not wish to go astray with those blind men, must look beyond works, and laws and doctrines about works; nay, turning his eyes from works, he must look upon the person, and ask how that is justified. For the person is justified and saved not by works nor by laws, but by the Word of God, that is, by the promise of His grace, and by faith, that the glory may remain God's, Who saved us not by works of righteousness which we have done, but according to His mercy by the word of His grace, when we believed.

—Martin Luther

— ◆ ◆ ◆ —

Ignatius of Loyola (1491–1556)

Spiritual Exercises

A book of devotions and guided meditations for the development of the spiritual life. One of the methods which Ignatius suggests is the exercise of imagining yourself present at the events recorded in the Gospels. Many moderns have found this guide still useful in the twentieth century.

John Calvin (1509–1564)

Institutes of the Christian Religion

Calvin is the other great Reformer and a man of penetrating intelligence. His *Institutes* are indisputably one of the
most important of all works of theology. They evidence his
attempt to formulate a logical and systematic presentation of
all the areas of theology. Comparing Calvin himself with the
popular conception of "Calvinism" might prove an eye-opening
experience for many readers. No one can deny his influence
on the development of theology.

◆ ◆ ◆

Our wisdom, in so far as it ought to be deemed true
and solid wisdom, consists almost entirely of two
parts—the knowledge of God and of ourselves. But
as these are connected together by many ties, it is
not easy to determine which of the two precedes and
gives birth to the other. For, in the first place, no man
can survey himself without forthwith turning his
thought toward the God in whom he lives and
moves. . . . The miserable ruin into which the revolt
of the first man has plunged us compels us to turn
our eyes upwards. . . . Since nothing appears within
us or around us which is not tainted with very great
impurity, so long as we keep our mind within the
confines of human pollution, anything which is in
some small degree less defiled delights us as if it
were most pure.

—John Calvin, *Institutes of the Christian Religion*

◆ ◆ ◆

Teresa of Avila (1515–1582)

Interior Castle
The Way of Perfection

A Spanish nun and mystic, Teresa's work is characterized by a deep devotion and a strong streak of practicality. Hers is a mysticism that can be practiced by the common man or woman. Note especially her warnings against false forms of spiritual experience. A wise book by a wise woman.

John of the Cross (1542–1591)

The Dark Night of the Soul
The Ascent of Mt. Carmel

A Spanish mystic with a poetic soul and an insight into the realities of the Christian experience. John is searchingly honest about the difficulties and ambiguities of the walk of faith. Difficult but essential reading for understanding the depth of Christian mysticism

William Shakespeare (1546–1616)

King Lear
The Merchant of Venice
Romeo and Juliet
Henry IV, parts 1 and 2
Hamlet
Macbeth
Othello

Whatever the circumstances of his personal life, it is unquestionably true that Shakespeare wrote from a Christian worldview. His insights on human will, guilt, forgiveness, and the search for truth should be required reading for every believer. His grasp of the human condition is perhaps unmatched in literature. If read seriously, his work becomes a mirror through which we can see ourselves. As the great critic Harold Bloom has written, "He perceived more than any other writer, thought more profoundly and originally than any other, and had an almost effortless mastery of language, far surpassing everyone."

Lancelot Andrewes (1555–1626)

Private Devotions

The lovely poetic meditations of an Anglican cleric, whose style helped form the *Book of Common Prayer*. A cadence at once both lofty and heartfelt is struck in this series of devotional prayers.

Jacobus Arminius (1560–1609)

The Declaration of Sentiments

If Calvin's *Institutes* are the classic statement of Calvinistic theology, this is the classic statement of the Arminian branch of theology, which emphasizes the freedom of man to respond to God.

Francis de Sales (1567–1622)

Introduction to the Devout Life

This book offers advice on holy living that influenced generations of Protestants and Catholics alike. A treasure trove of spiritual jewels. This is no otherworldly mysticism, but a practical and challenging guidebook to spiritual growth.

John Donne (1575–1631)

Selections from his sermons
Poems

Don't miss the work of this craftsman of the English language and master poet. His poems manage to crystallize spiritual experiences and communicate the drama of an encounter with God.

———————————— ♦♦♦ ————————————

Batter my heart, three-personed God; for You
As yet but knock, breathe, shine, and seek to mend;
That I may rise, and stand, overthrow me, and bend
Your force, to break, blow, burn and make me new.
I, like a usurped town, to another due,
Labor to admit You but Oh, to no end!
Reason, Your viceroy in me, should defend,
But it is captive, and proves weak or untrue.
Yet dearly I love You, and would be loved fain.
But am betrothed unto Your enemy;
Divorce me, untie, or break that knot again,
Take me to You, imprison me, for I
Except You enthrall me, never shall be free,
Nor ever chaste, except You ravish me.

—John Donne, *Divine Sonnets*

———————————— ♦♦♦ ————————————

George Herbert (1593–1633)

Poems

Simple but honest and beautiful poems, mostly about the spiritual life. Part of the strength of Herbert's poetry is that he does not, as many religious poets do, tell us how we should feel, but rather is honest about the struggles we all face. His love for the Savior is unmistakable.

— ♦♦♦ —

Love bade me welcome; yet my soul drew back,
    Guilty of dust and sin.
But quick-eyed love, observing me grow slack
    From my first entrance in,
Drew nearer to me, sweetly questioning,
    If I lacked any thing.

A guest, I answered, worthy to be here;
    Love said, You shall be he.
I the unkind, ungrateful? Ah my dear,
    I cannot look on thee.
Love took my hand, and smiling did reply,
    Who made the eyes but I?

Truth Lord, but I have marred them: let my shame
    Go where it doth deserve.
And know you not says Love, who bore the blame?
    My dear then I will serve.
You must sit down, says Love, and taste my meat;
    So I did sit down and eat.

—George Herbert, "Love"

John Milton (1608–1674)

Paradise Lost
Poems

The great epic *Paradise Lost* is a bold, dramatic re-creation of the fall of man. One of the most important poems of all time and influential in creating some of our popular cultural conceptions of God and the devil.

Brother Lawrence (1611–1691)

The Practice of the Presence of God

The writings of a simple monk who learned to live moment by moment in the presence of God despite the distractions of life. A life-transforming work that stresses the reality of relationship with the living God.

Richard Baxter (1615–1691)

The Saints' Everlasting Rest

The great Puritan writer calls us to form our lives in recognition of the life hereafter, which is only available to those who trust completely in the grace of God. A work of concrete hope based on the promises and character of God.

Blaise Pascal (1623–1662)

Pensées

Pensées is the French word for "thoughts," and that is what this collection of writings consists of. This is a gathering of thoughts in preparation for a book on the truth of the

Christian faith. Pascal died before the book could be published, but he left behind a gathering of jottings on the nature of man, the reality of God, and the paradox of faith—issues so current that the book reads as though it could have been written yesterday. An intelligent book on the limits of reason and the necessity of faith.

———————————— ♦ ♦ ♦ ————————————

Reason's last step is the recognition that there are an infinite number of things which are beyond it. It is merely feeble if it does not go as far as to realize that.

The heart has reasons of which reason knows nothing.

Knowing God without knowing our own wretchedness makes for pride. Knowing our wretchedness without knowing God makes for despair. Knowing Jesus Christ strikes the balance because he shows us both God and our own wretchedness.

—Blaise Pascal, *Pensées*

———————————— ♦ ♦ ♦ ————————————

George Fox (1624–1691)

Journal

The journal of the great Quaker social activist and spiritual leader. His life is an example of how powerful one man's life can be when he devotes himself to living by the principles of Jesus Christ, even when this goes "against the flow" of the prevailing religious establishment.

John Bunyan (1628–1688)

The Pilgrim's Progress

One of the most-loved books of all time, *Pilgrim's Progress* is an allegorical story that parallels the journey of faith of the Christian. Many of its images are unforgettable, and its vision of the Christian life is realistic and ultimately filled with great hope.

———————— ◆◆◆ ————————

[Christian] ran thus till he came to a place somewhat ascending; and upon that place stood a cross and a little below in the bottom, a sepulcher. So I saw in my dream, that just as Christian came up with the cross, his burden loosed from off his shoulders and fell from off his back, and began to tumble and so continued to do till it came to the mouth of the sepulcher, where it fell in and I saw it no more.

—John Bunyan, *The Pilgrim's Progress*

———————— ◆◆◆ ————————

Phillip Jakob Spener (1635–1705)

Pia Desideria

Puritan reflections on the life of faith. Spener argues that the church needs reformation and that this will only come through a renewed emphasis on the Bible, the priesthood of all believers, true Christian lifestyle, and holiness among the clergy. This still sounds like a good prescription today.

Thomas Traherne (1637–1674)

Centuries of Meditations

Prose poems which show evidence of deep faith and an appreciation for nature as the creation of God. Traherne sees the majesty of God filling and enriching all of creation. This book, largely forgotten, deserves to be better known than it is. This is some of the most beautiful writing in the English language.

---------------- ♦ ♦ ♦ ----------------

You never enjoy the world aright, till you see how a grain of sand exhibiteth the wisdom and power of God, and prize in every thing the service which they do to you in manifesting His glory and goodness to your soul far more than the visible beauty of their surface, or the material services they can do your body.

Your enjoyment of the world is never right till every morning you awake in your Father's palace and look upon the skies and the earth and the air as celestial joys having such a reverend esteem of all, as if you were among the angels. The bride of a monarch, in her husband's chamber, hath no such causes of delight as you.

—Thomas Traherne, *Centuries of Meditations*

---------------- ♦ ♦ ♦ ----------------

Madame Jeanne Guyon (1648–1717)

Experiencing the Depths of Jesus Christ

A guide to prayer which emphasizes the necessity of self-abnegation and radical abandonment to the will of God. A key work of the Quietist school of spirituality.

Francis Fénelon (1651–1715)

Christian Perfection

Fénelon is a French spiritual writer who discusses all phases of the spiritual life, with a focus on humility and trust in God to transform our lives. His advice was much-sought and cherished in his own time and remains powerful today.

Daniel Defoe (1660–1731)

Robinson Crusoe

The famous novel of a shipwrecked man who tries to cope with life outside civilization. Crusoe learns the necessity of trust in the providence of God to care for him. An engaging and exciting story

The Eighteenth Century

These years brought about the first concentrated challenge to the earlier dominance of Christianity in the intellectual sphere. Enlightenment thinkers did not flinch from bringing the truths of the Scriptures into question. Christian thinkers, meanwhile, tended to turn inside, focusing on the interior life. The majority of the Christian works of this period emphasize the relationship of the individual believer with Christ. Christians were experiencing a time of revival, renewal, and spiritual refreshment, even in the face of this intellectual struggle. However, the failure to adequately address the objections raised during this time may be the reason for the gradual decline in the cultural impact of Christianity.

◆◆◆

Jonathan Swift (1667–1745)

Gulliver's Travels

In *Gulliver's Travels*, Swift, a cleric with an acerbic wit, demonstrates his disbelief in the perfectibility of human nature. Though one can read this book simply as an exciting adventure tale, it is much more than that. Swift can also be read as a critic of the new Enlightenment ideas that were sweeping Europe in his time. He lays bare the corrupt nature of man and his inadequacy for designing a society based on reason and order. Swift's other satiric tales, including *A Modest Proposal* and *Battle of the Books,* further demonstrate his great intelligence and caustic sense of humor.

Jean Paul de Caussade (c. 1675–1751)

Abandonment to Divine Providence

A gem of a book expressing a deep trust of God's sovereign superintendence of our lives. Every moment, says Caussade, is a sacred opportunity to allow God to shape and change us by the experiences that come our way. The spirit of the book is captured well in Kitty Muggeridge's translation entitled *The Sacrament of the Present Moment.*

William Law (1686–1761)

A Serious Call to the Devout and Holy Life

A classic Anglican work of devotion, characterized by its levelheadedness and practicality. C. S. Lewis is among those who feel it is one of the handful of truly great books on spiritual living.

Jonathan Edwards (1703–1758)

Treatise on Religious Affections

One of the most important theologians of the eighteenth century, Edwards writes on the place of emotions in the spiritual life. As with his other works, this book is characterized by a deep reliance on Scripture and a systematic intelligence. Many will argue that Edwards was one of the most brilliant minds that the United States has ever produced. Along with his powerful sermons, Edwards also produced books on practical spirituality and on philosophy. In recent years, there has been a resurgence of interest from the academic community in Edwards's careful philosophical writings. Edwards's heart, however, was always fired by a passion for the revival of vigorous faith in the heart of the believer.

John Gerstner has produced a slim, readable volume outlining Edwards's theological system.

———————————— ♦♦♦ ————————————

As in worldly things worldly affections are very much the spring of men's motions and action; so in religious matters the spring of their actions is very much religious affections. He that has doctrinal knowledge and speculation only, without affection, never is engaged in the business of religion. Nothing is more manifest, in fact, than that the things of religion take hold of men's souls no further than they affect them.

— Jonathan Edwards, *Treatise on Religious Affections*

———————————— ♦♦♦ ————————————

John Wesley (1703–1791)

Journal

Probably the best source for understanding the thought and motivations of the founder of Methodism. Wesley broke through much of the dry scholasticism of his time and emerged with a faith based on a "heart strangely warmed."

———————————— ♦♦♦ ————————————

In the evening I went very unwillingly to a society in Aldersgate Street, where one was reading Luther's preface to the Epistle to the Romans. About a quarter before nine, while he was describing the change

which God works in the heart through faith in Christ,
I felt my heart strangely warmed. I felt I did trust
Christ alone, for salvation. And an assurance was
given me that he had taken away my sins, even
mine, and saved me from the law of sin and death.

—John Wesley, *Journal*

◆◆◆

David Brainerd (1718–1747)

Diary

This is the stirring diary of a true man of prayer. A missionary to the American Indians, Brainerd's effectiveness arose from the astonishing amount of time he spent on his knees. A book guaranteed to awaken an awareness of our own lack of prayer and to call us to spend more time with our loving Father.

William Blake (1757–1827)

Songs of Innocence
Songs of Experience

Though his theological outlook was far from orthodox, Blake's poetry contains a vigorous evocation of the difference that having eyes of faith makes in viewing the world. His poetry is, at times, disarmingly simple on the surface, but is constructed around a deeply held belief in an order beyond the world of things. Blake's poetry was original and highly influential on succeeding generations.

The Nineteenth Century

This was a period of great challenges to the church. In response to attacks from prominent intellectuals (Marx, Comte, Nietzsche, etc.) and the general feeling that Christianity was becoming irrelevant, Christian thinkers struggled to make their faith intelligible to the modern mind. Many reformulated the gospel to make it more acceptable to its despisers, thus giving birth to liberal theology. Others emphasized the emotional promise of the gospel or wedded it to political agendas. Still others met the challenge by engaging the modern mind in new and creative ways while remaining faithful to "the faith once delivered."

Friedrich Schleiermacher (1768–1834)

On Religion: Speeches to Its Cultured Despisers

Schleiermacher attempted to communicate Christianity to his peers in the Romantic movement, and to describe the life of faith in a way that could be grasped without recourse to dogmatic theological statements. Both his conception of religion as "the feeling of absolute dependence" and his theological method have had a profound effect on liberal theology. His prose is dense and difficult.

Samuel Taylor Coleridge (1772–1834)

Poems
Aids to Reflection

One of the leaders of the Romantic movement, a literary critic and amateur theologian as well as a poet, Coleridge is a figure to be reckoned with. A convert to Christianity whose poems often demonstrate an interest in the things of the spirit.

Charles Finney (1792–1875)

Lectures on Revivals of Religion

An important forerunner of the evangelical movement, Finney called for a commitment that was radical and whole-hearted. He recognized the important place of the emotions in the Christian life, but was, most of all, utterly committed to the Bible and its message.

John Henry Newman (1801–1890)

Apologia Pro Vita Sua

The beautifully written story of Newman's conversion from Anglicanism to Catholicism. Newman was an astute theologian and one of the most important Catholic thinkers of modern times.

Nikolai Gogol (1809–1852)

Short Stories
Dead Souls

Gogol wrote rather strange and nightmarish stories about the human inability to make sense of an absurd world. He had tremendous insight into the hollowness of a society constructed without God.

Robert Browning (1812–1889)

Poems

The intensity of Browning's faith shows itself in many of his poems. He is the rare poet who can write of spiritual things in such a way that they communicate even to the unbeliever.

Sören Kierkegaard (1813–1855)

Either/Or
Fear and Trembling
Sickness Unto Death
Training in Christianity
The Attack Upon Christendom

One of the profoundest thinkers of modern times, Kierkegaard saw the human predicament clearly: that human beings could not find the meaning and depth of their existence by the use of reason alone. Rather, it is only the life of faith that allows us to reach our full personhood and to give our lives purpose. This faith must be one of absolute commitment, even when it appears irrational. One cannot overstate Kierkegaard's influence on thinkers of various stripes. A good introduction to his often difficult thought is Robert Bretall's *A Kierkegaard Anthology*, which includes excellent notes. Also of interest is Walter Lowrie's biography, *A Short Life of Kierkegaard*.

◆◆◆

The thing is to understand myself, to see what God really wishes me to do; the thing is to find a truth which is really true for me, and to find the idea for which I can live and die. . . . What good would it do me to be able to explain the meaning of Christianity if it had no deeper significance for me and for my life;—what good would it do me if truth stood before me, cold and naked, not caring whether I recognized

her or not, and producing in me a shudder of fear
rather than a trusting devotion?

—Sören Kierkegaard, *Journals*

————————————— ◆ ◆ ◆ —————————————

Anthony Trollope (1815–1882)

The Warden
Barchester Towers

Charming tales of rural clerical life which show keen
insight into human nature. Both touching and humorous,
these books are only the first two in a series of novels about
the politics of a parish. Pastors and priests will recognize
how little things have changed when it comes to the internal
battles of church politics.

Anonymous Russian Monk

The Way of a Pilgrim

This key work of the Russian spiritual tradition teaches
the use of the Jesus Prayer, a way of "praying unceasingly."
This spiritual discipline has influenced countless believers in
the Orthodox tradition and elsewhere.

Fyodor Dostoevski (1821–1881)

The Underground Man
Crime and Punishment
The Idiot
The Brothers Karamazov

Dostoevski is quite possibly the greatest novelist of all
time. His novels, especially *The Brothers Karamazov*, deal

with the entire gamut of human emotions and religious experience. He struggles with an array of intellectual and spiritual issues, but never lets the story itself bog down. Dostoevski's writing demonstrates a haunting awareness of the depths to which human beings can sink and the heights of self-sacrifice of which we are capable. And he tells it all with a passion that puts most other novelists to shame. Here is the Christian worldview demonstrated at its most profound with passages of awe-inspiring beauty.

------------------------------ ♦♦♦ ------------------------------

The awful thing is that beauty is mysterious as well as terrible. God and the devil are fighting there, and the battlefield is the heart of man.

—Fyodor Dostoevski, *The Brothers Karamazov*

------------------------------ ♦♦♦ ------------------------------

George MacDonald (1824–1903)

Fairy Tales
Lilith
At the Back of the North Wind
Thomas Wingfold, Curate

With a romantic's zest for life and appreciation of nature, and a childlike sense of the truly important, George MacDonald presents a view of human life that is perhaps most notable for its rich sense of holiness. All of his writing reveals a man in love with his present existence who, at the same time, longs for eternity. His fairy tales and novels contain, despite their imperfections, many of the most powerful moments of spiritual insight in literature. MacDonald deeply influenced later writers such as C. S. Lewis. Both Michael Phillips and Roland Hein have written interesting biographical studies, and Hein's literary study, *The Harmony Within,* is indispensable. Most of the novels have been edited for contemporary readers by Michael Phillips and assigned different titles.

Leo Tolstoy (1828–1910)

War and Peace
Anna Karenina
The Death of Ivan Ilyich
Short Stories
My Confession

Tolstoy and Dostoevski are the two giants of Russian literature. Tolstoy's ability to create memorable characters and to graphically show how real change takes place within the hearts and souls of his characters are two of the many things that make his novels so great. Short-story parables such as "How Much Land Does a Man Need?" or "Master and Man" are a good place to begin exploring the world of Tolstoy. Although his personal theology was less than orthodox, he saw deeply into the failures of man as compared with the splendid example of Jesus Christ. *My Confession* is a powerful book about his own religious awakening.

Hannah Whitall Smith (1832–1911)

The Christian's Secret of a Happy Life

A simple exploration of the joys of Christian faith which still retains its popularity. A call to complete dependence and unflinching holiness.

Charles Spurgeon (1834–1892)

John Ploughman's Talks
Sermons

One of the greatest masters of the pulpit, with a brilliant mind and dedication to the Scriptures, Spurgeon could hold audiences spellbound with his rhetoric, his metaphors, and his intense passion for lost souls. All these come out in his sermons and writings.

Gerard Manley Hopkins (1844–1889)

Poems

Hopkins had a keen eye for the beauties of nature, and the ability to use his mastery of the English language to produce beautiful poetry. Characterized by his desire to glimpse into the very nature of things (which he called "inscape"), Hopkins's work employs a striking juxtaposition of words to produce a rhythm that gives the poems their originality. One of my favorite poets.

———————————————— ◆◆◆ ————————————————

The world is charged with the grandeur of God.
    It will flame out, like shining from shook foil;
    It gathers to a greatness, like the ooze of oil
Crushed. Why do men then now not reck his rod?
Generations have trod, have trod, have trod;
    And all is seared with trade, bleared, smeared
      with toil;

And wears man's smudge and shares man's
   smell: the soil
Is bare now, nor can foot feel, being shod.

And for all this, nature is never spent;
   There lives the dearest freshness deep down
      things;
And though the last lights off the black west went
   Oh morning, at the brown brink eastward,
      springs—
Because the Holy Ghost over the bent
   World broods with warm breast and with ah!
      bright wings.

> —Gerard Manley Hopkins, "God's Grandeur"

—————————— ♦ ♦ ♦ ——————————

Charles Sheldon (1857–1946)

In His Steps

A popular novel about a church that undertakes a life-changing experiment: making no choices in life without first asking, "What would Jesus do?" The results make for truly inspiring and challenging reading.

Francis Thompson (1859–1907)

Poems

Thompson finds a place on this list largely on the strength of his remarkable poem "The Hound of Heaven," which provides an unforgettable picture of God's passionate pursuit of the human soul. God's love causes Him never to despair of us or give up on us.

———————————— ♦♦♦ ————————————

I fled Him, down the nights and down the days;
I fled Him, down the arches of the years;
I fled Him, down the labyrinthine ways
   Of my own mind; and in the mist of tears
I hid from Him, and under running laughter.
     Up vistaed hopes I sped;
     And shot, precipitated,
Adown Titanic glooms of chasmed fears,
From those strong Feet that followed,
     followed after.
        —Francis Thompson, "The Hound of Heaven"

———————————— ♦♦♦ ————————————

Amy Carmichael (1867–1951)

If

Amy Carmichael dedicated her life to improving the lot and saving the souls of young girls made temple prostitutes in India. Much of the simple love and trust which marked her life is demonstrated also in her writing, like this book of simple but profound meditations. The biography by Elisabeth Elliot (*A Chance to Die*) is valuable for understanding her accomplishments.

Thérèse of Lisieux (1873–1897)

The Story of a Soul

The simple and tender story of a very young French nun whose love for God knew no bounds. Although Protestants may find elements of her story (her extreme asceticism, for example) off-putting, no one can help but be struck by her passion for and devotion to the Lord Jesus Christ. "The little flower," as she is commonly known, is one of the most popular of modern saints.

Oswald Chambers (1874–1917)

My Utmost for His Highest

This book of daily devotional readings has continued to find readers well into our own time. Chambers's powerful reflections are based upon deep evangelical experience and a close study of the Scriptures.

The Twentieth Century

With the loss of confidence in absolute truth in modern times, Christianity has become just one more voice competing for attention in the marketplace of ideas. Failing to recognize how much it owes to the Christian tradition, our culture has increasingly cast aside many of those elements that made our culture what it is. Perhaps, though, the fact that Christianity is no longer the central belief system of our culture gives us the opportunity to speak in clearer and more powerful ways, as it is not so easy to confuse the Christian faith with our modern cultural religion. As "cultural religiosity" falters in its impact on twentieth-century people, the radical imperatives of the gospel of grace can perhaps penetrate the religious veneer of the western world and strike deeply into our hearts. Certainly a number of writers of great skill and insight have taken up this challenge.

◆◆◆

G. K. Chesterton (1874–1936)

Orthodoxy
The Everlasting Man
The Man Who Was Thursday
The Father Brown Stories

"The Shakespeare of the aphorism" is the title that someone has given to Gilbert Keith Chesterton. Chesterton had the ability to pack more paradox and more truth into a single sentence than possibly any writer in history. This characteristic makes his books a joy to read for their penetrating insight and their infectious cleverness. Put this together with a swashbuckling faith, a warm and joyous sense of humor, and a dependence on plain common sense, and you have a fine definition of Chesterton's highly individual gift. It is a tough call to say which is best: his highly original nonfiction (*Orthodoxy, The Everlasting Man*) or his always-entertaining fiction (*Father Brown, The Man Who Was Thursday*). Either way, read both for a model of a man who enjoyed his faith.

——————————— ♦ ♦ ♦ ———————————

Because children have abounding vitality, because they are in spirit fierce and free, therefore they want things repeated and unchanged. They always say, "Do it again"; and the grown-up person does it again until he is nearly dead. For grown-up people are not strong enough to exult in monotony. It is possible that God says every morning, "Do it again" to the sun; and every evening, "Do it again" to the moon. It may not be automatic necessity that makes all daisies alike; it may be that God makes every daisy separately, but has never got tired of making them. It may be that He has the eternal appetite of infancy; for we have sinned and grown old, and our Father is younger than we. The repetition in Nature may not be a mere recurrence; it may be a theatrical encore.

—G. K. Chesterton, *Orthodoxy*

——————————— ♦ ♦ ♦ ———————————

Evelyn Underhill (1875–1941)

Mysticism

The definitive study of mysticism and its manifestations, written with great sympathy by a woman who was herself a mystic of note. This is the book to begin with if you wish to study the phenomenon of mysticism.

John Gresham Machen (1881–1937)

Christianity and Liberalism

A fearless defender of orthodox Christianity in a time when it appeared that theological liberalism would take the day, Machen's fiery passion is tempered by an exceedingly astute mind and a generosity of spirit. Those of us who call ourselves theological conservatives owe him a great debt of gratitude for his clarion call to the church in the early part of this century.

Pierre Teilhard de Chardin (1881–1955)

The Phenomenon of Man
The Divine Milieu

Teilhard was a French priest with an expertise in paleontology who tried to combine the key tenets of evolutionary theory with the teachings of the church. Although he was officially censured and silenced by the church, his mystical vision of cosmic spiritual evolution has continued to be very influential. Whatever conclusion you draw about his orthodoxy, his writings are both highly original and intriguing. For some, he is one of the greatest of modern mystics; to others, a heretical forerunner to modern "cosmic consciousness" and "New Age" thinking. Either way, his influence is undeniable.

Jacques Maritain (1882–1973)

True Humanism

One of the key works of this French philosopher, this book attempts to demonstrate that Christianity is the truest form of humanism. Maritain is never easy to read, but there is much insight to be drawn from his dense philosophical prose.

Rudolf Bultmann (1884–1976)

Jesus Christ and Mythology

Bultmann is known best for his project of "demythologization"—the stripping of the Gospel accounts of all their mythic and supernatural content in the attempt to reach the core teachings of Jesus. Whether this is a powerful tool for making the gospel relevant to today's scientific mind-set or just another form of reductionism (my opinion) is for the reader to decide. C. S. Lewis might have said that Bultmann suffers from "chronological snobbery"—the tendency to judge the old in the light of the new. Indisputably, his work has had a huge influence on the way much of theology is approached in our century.

Francois Mauriac (1885–1970)

Thérèse Desqueyroux
Viper's Tangle

Searing, introspective novels about sin and grace by an award-winning French novelist, these novels far transcend the category of religious fiction. Mauriac uses the realities of the human condition as the springboard for his theological musings in fictional form.

Karl Barth (1886–1968)

Church Dogmatics
The Word of God and the Word of Man

One of the major names in contemporary theology, Barth produced a shelf full of books on theological matters, including his multivolume *Church Dogmatics*. Barth founded his theology on the revelation of God in Jesus Christ. His writing is very learned and based upon careful exegesis of Scripture, yet has a freshness that makes his basic orthodoxy seem somehow unique and original. Geoffrey Bromiley has attempted to summarize Barth's ideas in *An Introduction to Karl Barth*, while Bernard Ramm's study of Barth, *After Fundamentalism*, will be of interest to evangelicals.

♦♦♦

Human thoughts about God do not constitute the content of the Bible; rather, it is the true divine thought about humanity. The Bible does not tell us how we should speak about God but what God says to us, not how we may find the way to him but how he has sought and found the way to us, not what is the proper relation in which we must stand to him but what is the covenant that he has made with all who in faith are the children of Abraham, and that he has sealed once and for all in Jesus Christ. This is what stands in the Bible.

—Karl Barth, *The Word of God and the Word of Man*

♦♦♦

Charles Williams (1886–1945)

Descent into Hell
The Place of the Lion
Descent of the Dove

A friend of C. S. Lewis and J. R. R. Tolkien, Williams produced a series of highly unusual novels characterized by their preoccupation with the inbreaking of the supernatural dimension into our world. They are filled with bizarre occurrences, moments of numinous revelation, and the depiction of intense spiritual experiences. Readers will find him either repellingly strange or utterly fascinating.

Paul Tillich (1886–1965)

The Courage to Be

Written by a controversial liberal theologian who was a great thinker and communicator, this book perhaps shows Tillich at his best, trying to communicate the gospel to the thoroughly modern individual. Even those who cannot agree with his theology will find his work full of insight and reflection.

T. S. Eliot (1888–1965)

The Wasteland
Ash Wednesday
The Rock
The Four Quartets
The Family Reunion
The Cocktail Party
Murder in the Cathedral

The finest modern poet and also a committed believer, T. S. Eliot captured so well the hopelessness of life without faith and the mysterious power of faith to transform lives and give meaning to human experience. I personally count reading *Four Quartets* among the most powerful spiritual experiences of my life. It is an almost inexhaustible source of profound meditation on time and eternity and their intersection in the present moment. Eliot is not always easy to read, but he is unquestionably worth the effort.

--------------------- ♦♦♦ ---------------------

Men's curiosity searches past and future
And clings to that dimension. But to apprehend
The point of intersection of the timeless
With time, is an occupation for the saint—
No occupation either, but something given
And taken, in a lifetime's death in love,
Ardour and selflessness and self-surrender.
For most of us, there is only the unattended
Moment, the moment in and out of time. . . .
These are only hints and guesses,
Hints followed by guesses; and the rest
Is prayer, observance, discipline, thought and action.
The hint half guessed, the gift half understood, is
    Incarnation.

                            —T. S. Eliot, *The Four Quartets*

--------------------- ♦♦♦ ---------------------

Georges Bernanos (1888–1948)

Diary of a Country Priest

A simple but beautiful tale of doubt, faith, and self-sacrifice. Bernanos's hero is a young priest whose life is riddled with self-doubt and questioning, but who nevertheless provides those around him with a powerful witness to the love and mercy of God. Some of the passages in this book are truly heart-wrenching.

Gabriel Marcel (1889–1973)

The Mystery of Being

The major work by this French Catholic philosopher, who agrees with modern existentialism that human existence is hard to make sense of, but emphasizes the difference between "life as a problem" (the view of most moderns) and "life as a mystery" (the Christian perspective). He criticizes Sartre's atheistic existentialism for its abstraction and its distance from the actual lives of human beings. Difficult, but worth the effort.

Boris Pasternak (1890–1960)

Doctor Zhivago

This powerful novel contains many Christian elements which are missing from the classic movie of the same name. Pasternak had a poet's touch in his descriptions of mood and place.

J. R. R. Tolkien (1892–1973)

The Hobbit
The Lord of the Rings trilogy

The immensely popular works of Tolkien can be read on two levels: 1) as very exciting and moving adventure tales, or 2) as a personal mythology which is deeply indebted to

Norse mythology, Arthurian legend, and the Christian gospel. These are gripping tales of heroism, loyalty, courage, and sacrifice. But even more, they are a strong testimony to the providence of God and the hope of the ultimate triumph of good over evil. To better understand their religious underpinnings, read Tolkien's more difficult (but very rewarding) epic, *The Silmarillion,* and the fine biography by Humphrey Carpenter.

Reinhold Niebuhr (1892–1971)

Leaves from the Notebook of a Tamed Cynic
Moral Man and Immoral Society
The Nature and Destiny of Man

One of the most important American theologians, Niebuhr combined a deep passion for social justice, a strong grasp of intellectual history, and a profound sense of human sinfulness and finiteness. His writing is lively and honest enough that in his own time it gained him many followers, even among those who could not accept his theology.

Thomas Kelly (1893–1941)

A Testament of Devotion

From the Quaker tradition, Kelly delivers a call for simplicity, inner silence, and the necessity for attuning one's heart and spirit to the voice of God. A book that deserves a slow and meditative reading.

Dorothy L. Sayers (1893–1957)

The Man Born to Be King
The Mind of the Maker
Christian Letters to a Post-Christian World
Creed or Chaos

The author of the popular *Lord Peter Wimsey* detective novels was also the writer of wonderful religious dramas (*The Man Born to Be King* is a magnificent drama covering the life of Christ) and witty apologetic writings. Sayers stressed the parallel between the image of God as seen in human creativity and the creativity of the Creator. She was firmly convinced of the reasonableness of orthodox Christianity and was one of its most able modern defenders.

H. Richard Niebuhr (1894–1962)

Christ and Culture

A very suggestive and important study of the various ways of relating Christ to culture. Absolutely essential reading for anyone interested in the question of how we can integrate our faith with the modern world.

A. W. Tozer (1897–1963)

The Pursuit of God

Tozer manages to break out of the cliché-ridden lingo that characterizes much of the evangelical writing on the spiritual life. What emerges is a book notable for its depth of insight into the human spirit and for the single-hearted passion of its author for the Savior. Magnificent!

---------------- ◆◆◆ ----------------

To have found God and still to pursue Him is the
soul's paradox of love, scorned indeed by the
too-easily-satisfied religionist, but justified in happy
experience by the children of the burning heart. . . .

    Come near to the holy men and women of the
past and you will soon feel the heat of their desire
after God. They mourned for Him, they prayed and
wrestled and sought for Him day and night, in season
and out, and when they had found Him the finding
was all the sweeter for the long seeking.

—A. W. Tozer, *The Pursuit of God*

---------------- ◆◆◆ ----------------

C. S. Lewis (1898–1963)

Mere Christianity
The Screwtape Letters
The Great Divorce
The Abolition of Man
The Chronicles of Narnia
The Space Trilogy
Till We Have Faces
The Weight of Glory and Other Essays

Perhaps no other writer of the twentieth century has
done more for the cause of orthodox Christian faith than
Clive Staples Lewis. His combination of a vigorous commitment to the reasonableness of faith and his soaring creativity
produced a body of work that gives hope to the modern person who finds so many modern pronouncements of faith to

be sterile and mindless. For me personally, his work is a veritable lifeline thrown into a Christian subculture that is so often intellectually and creatively stagnant. By all means do not miss reading Lewis, and don't stop with the list given above. These titles are just a sample of the rewarding reading experiences Lewis offers.

———————————— ♦ ♦ ♦ ————————————

At present we are on the outside of the world, the wrong side of the door. We discern the freshness and purity of morning, but they do not make us fresh and pure. We cannot mingle with the splendours we see. But all the leaves of the New Testament are rustling with the rumour that it will not always be so. Some day, God willing, we shall get in. . . .

It is a serious thing to live in a society of possible gods and goddesses, to remember that the dullest and most uninteresting person you talk to may one day be a creature which, if you saw it now, you would be strongly tempted to worship, or else a horror and corruption such as you now meet, if at all, only in a nightmare. All day long we are, in some degree, helping each other to one or other of these destinations. It is in the light of these overwhelming possibilities, it is with the awe and circumspection proper to them, that we should conduct all our dealings with one another, all friendships, all loves, all play, all politics. There are no ordinary people.

—C. S. Lewis, "The Weight of Glory"

———————————— ♦ ♦ ♦ ————————————

Ignazio Silone (1900–1978)

Bread and Wine

An excellent novel by an Italian Catholic writer who struggles with the relationship of faith and politics in Fascist Italy during the years surrounding the Second World War. An unbeliever, disguised as a priest to avoid persecution, finds his life and attitudes slowly changing. Silone's insights into politics make this an important and fascinating read.

Evelyn Waugh (1903–1966)

A Handful of Dust
Brideshead Revisited

A deft comic touch marks all the work of this important British novelist. His constant theme is the vacuity of life without God. Rather than concentrating on the joys of faith, this talented curmudgeon emphasizes the boredom and stifling meaninglessness of the life that is focused on this world's attractions. A powerful critique of modern aimlessness and at the same time an absolutely tremendous read. These two novels are marked by beautiful writing, wry humor, and a painfully accurate depiction of the desperateness of the human condition.

Malcolm Muggeridge (1903–1990)

Jesus Rediscovered
The End of Christendom
Something Beautiful for God

Muggeridge was a British journalist who became, late in life, a convert to Catholicism. Muggeridge is in many ways the archetypical curmudgeon: skeptical, cranky, and dryly humorous. But his best work also evidences an unexpected tenderness and passion. He was a fearless defender of Christian truth and a writer of amazing clarity and style. His book *The Third Testament* reveals those who influenced him the most: Kierkegaard, Pascal, Blake, and Dostoevski, among others. To say that he is worthy company for these greats is to give an idea of his own talent and originality.

Graham Greene (1904–1991)

The Power and the Glory
The Heart of the Matter
The End of the Affair
Monsignor Quixote

Greene is almost universally acknowledged as one of the great novelists of the twentieth century. His books often center around spiritual themes which he unfolds with insight, suspense, and authenticity. Many of Greene's books catch human beings attempting to hold on to some shred of faith in an extremely dark situation. They testify to the difficulty of the life of faith and trumpet the virtues of loyalty and courage. Most of his books demonstrate his unusual ability to create not only vivid characters but also to produce an unforgettable atmosphere wherein the story unfolds (some have jokingly referred to it as "Greeneland"). His best-known work is probably *The Power and the Glory* about an alcoholic priest on the run in Mexico at a time when Christianity is outlawed and all priests are being systematically eliminated.

Pursued by an upright law officer, who is an atheist, the priest struggles against his own faltering faith and the unrelenting pursuit of the police. The priest's heroic demise is testimony to the strength of the gospel, even in the face of our flaws. *Monsignor Quixote* is a lighter and funnier but equally evocative tale.

Dietrich Bonhoeffer (1906–1945)

> *The Cost of Discipleship*
> *Life Together*   .
> *Letters and Papers from Prison*

Bonhoeffer has been interpreted in many differing ways by people from every part of the theological spectrum. The one thing that is indisputable is that he was a gifted and original thinker and a courageous human being. At a time when many in Germany made concessions to the Nazi regime, Bonhoeffer stood strong and true for the integrity of the gospel. He worked to thwart the plans of Hitler and to strengthen the underground church. When he was offered safety in America, he chose to return to Germany to stand with his countrymen. In the end, he was executed by the Nazis just a few days before the camp where he spent his last days was liberated by the Allies. Many of his ideas are critical to the modern theological dialogue: "the world come of age," "religionless Christianity," "cheap grace," and "costly grace," to name a few. He causes us to think deeply about what it means to live as a Christian in the twentieth century. Here was a man of passion, conviction, and gentle spirituality whose life story is as inspiring as his work.

The Cost of Discipleship is a study of the meaning of true grace and a reflection on the Sermon on the Mount. *Life*

Together is a rich study of the spiritual life and community. It is full of wise advice on growing spiritually. *Letters and Papers from Prison* is a collection of his last writings and the profound reflections on life and faith which occupied his mind during his last days. The biography by Eberhard Bethge is a classic study by a close friend.

━━━━━━━━━━━━━━ ◆ ◆ ◆ ━━━━━━━━━━━━━━

Cheap grace is the preaching of forgiveness without requiring repentance, baptism without church discipline, communion without confession, absolution without personal confession. Cheap grace is grace without discipleship, grace without the cross, grace without Jesus Christ, living and incarnate. . . .

[Costly] grace is costly because it calls us to follow, and it is grace because it calls us to follow Jesus Christ. It is costly because it costs a man his life, and it is grace because it gives a man the only true life. It is costly because it condemns sin, and grace because it justifies the sinner. Above all, it is costly because it cost God the life of his Son.

—Dietrich Bonhoeffer, *The Cost of Discipleship*

━━━━━━━━━━━━━━ ◆ ◆ ◆ ━━━━━━━━━━━━━━

W. H. Auden (1907–1973)

Poems

A thoroughly modern poet, Auden believed that only the Christian faith held the real truth about our lives. He wrote powerful poems on many topics (and was a fine essayist as well) and had the ability to create phrases that remain in the consciousness long after his books have been returned to the shelf.

Helmut Thielicke (1908–1985)

The Waiting Father
Theological Ethics

Thielicke deserves to be much more well-known among American evangelicals than he is. He was a German theologian who had that rarest of gifts: the ability to communicate orthodoxy in a way that is intellectually satisfying and yet takes into account the difficult hurdles that the modern skeptic must overcome to believe. His wide-ranging intellect, demonstrated over the entirety of his work, is staggering. He seems to have read and reflected on nearly everything of importance, and his conclusions are both orthodox and fresh at the same time. His talent for delivering sermons made him a hero in postwar Germany, where people flocked to hear the gospel preached by this courageous and talented man.

The Waiting Father demonstrates his gift as a preacher and expositor as he reflects on the sermon of the prodigal son. His insights will astound and inspire you. *Theological Ethics* is one of his scholarly works and evidences careful thinking, exhaustive research, and spiritual depth.

Simone Weil (1909–1943)

Waiting for God

A spiritual pilgrim who was never able to feel comfortable in the established church, Weil identified with the needs and experiences of the common person and gave her life in a quiet heroism to that end. She died at a young age following her heroic efforts during World War II. Weil was a social activist, a scholar, and a writer of unusual ability. *Waiting for God* contains her spiritual reflections. Robert Coles, himself something of a kindred spirit to Weil, has written an insightful biography.

Walker Percy (1916–1990)

The Moviegoer
The Second Coming
Lost in the Cosmos: The Last Self-Help Book
The Thanatos Syndrome

Quite possibly my favorite modern novelist, Walker Percy brings a unique blend of scientific precision in observation, deep commitment to the Christian worldview, southern humor, and a vast intellect to his work. Percy's work focuses on the existential quandaries of the modern person and lays bare the aimlessness and ennui of our culture. As a cultural critic he is unparalleled, but that never gets in the way of creating a wonderful reading experience. And, oh is he funny! I would suggest *The Second Coming* (which has nothing to do with eschatology) as the best place to start exploring his work. Be forewarned that Percy is a thoroughly modern novelist and deals with issues of life in an unflinching and honest way. His frankness adds much to the overriding message of his work: Human beings cannot survive with sanity and truth unless God is granted His rightful place in their lives.

I highly recommend the excellent biography *Pilgrim in the Ruins* by Jay Toulson.

Francis Schaeffer (1912–1984)

> *The God Who Is There*
> *How Should We Then Live?*

When Francis Schaeffer's first works were published in the late 1960s, his was a voice that the evangelical church needed to hear. He called us to intellectual respectability, artistic integrity, and authentic Christian living. Time has shown that his insights were truly prophetic. He foresaw much of what was coming in terms of the growth of secularism and moral decay. Schaeffer desired to reach a mass audience with a philosophical message about the meaning of life and the truth of the Christian faith. Few have been so successful in this difficult goal. Schaeffer especially deserves applause for his encouragement of the arts and culture in the often anti-art evangelical subculture. The basic outlines of his thought are best captured in his "trilogy" (*The God Who Is There*, *Escape From Reason*, and *He Is There and He Is Not Silent*) and illustrated in his survey of modern history (*How Should We Then Live?*).

Thomas Merton (1915–1968)

> *The Seven Storey Mountain*
> *New Seeds of Contemplation*
> *Thoughts in Solitude*

A Trappist monk and devotional writer of great depth and wide appeal, Merton crystallizes the experience of the modern Christian for many of his fans. His best work arises out of his own concerns and struggles. Here is a modern odyssey of the spirit wedded with a writing ability that could have made him a considerable novelist. Richly contemplative.

Several good biographies exist about this major influence on modern spiritual life: Michael Mott's *The Seven Mountains of Thomas Merton,* Monica Furlong's *Thomas Merton,* and William H. Shannon's *Silent Lamp* (my favorite). All deal with the difficult question of Merton's late-in-life flirtation with Eastern thought.

──────────── ◆ ◆ ◆ ────────────

My Lord God, I have no idea where I am going. I do not see the road ahead of me. I cannot know for certain where it will end. Nor do I really know myself, and the fact that I think I am following your will does not mean I am actually doing so. But I believe that the desire to please you does in fact please you. And I hope I have that desire in all that I am doing. I hope that if I do this you will lead me by the right road, though I may know nothing about it. Therefore I will trust you always though I may seem to be lost and in the shadow of death. I will not fear, for you are ever with me, and you will never leave me to face my perils alone.

—Thomas Merton, *Thoughts in Solitude*

──────────── ◆ ◆ ◆ ────────────

Flannery O'Connor (1925–1964)

Wise Blood
Mystery and Manners
A Good Man Is Hard to Find
Everything That Rises Must Converge

Strange tales by a leading Southern novelist who was an unabashed believer. Many will find O'Connor's stories perplexing until they understand what she was trying to do: to shock the reader into a realization of his or her own sinfulness and self-deceit. These are the kind of stories that will haunt the reader's imagination long after he or she is finished with the book. *Mystery and Manners* discusses her Christian perspective on art and writing. Her unusual and unforgettable stories are not to be missed.

Martin Luther King (1929–1968)

Strength to Love

Besides being one of the most potent political figures of the twentieth century, Martin Luther King was an inspired orator, and this collection of writings captures his prophetic voice very well. Even a cursory perusal of his sermons will reveal the consistent presence of biblical imagery in his writings and orations. King's model was the prophetic tradition of the Old Testament, and his own thundering rhetoric is similarly filled with indignation, the promise of judgment, and the coming reign of righteousness.

Contemporaries . . .
Candidates for Greatness

Jacques Ellul

The Presence of the Kingdom
Prayer and Modern Man
The Technological Society

Ellul, a French theologian and sociologist, has written a number of books on the relationship between the Christian faith and modern society. His background in sociology affords many brilliant insights into contemporary society, written with the fire and courage of a biblical prophet. *Uncompromising, controversial,* and *provocative* are words that come quickly to mind when describing Ellul's work. A helpful introduction to his ideas can be found in a series of interviews published as a book entitled *In Season, Out of Season.*

Carl F. H. Henry

God, Revelation and Authority

Carl Henry is one of the great minds of modern evangelicalism, one of the founders of *Christianity Today* magazine, and one of the most vocal proponents of a more intellectually respectable proclamation of the gospel. His legacy to the evangelical community is immense.

God, Revelation and Authority is his massive statement of evangelical theology. Stretching to six fat volumes, Henry's work answers the objections of the critics against the authority and inerrancy of Scripture and restated traditional theology in an intellectually satisfying manner. It will undoubtedly be a landmark for future evangelical theologians.

Elisabeth Elliot

Through Gates of Splendour

The powerful narrative of Jim and Elisabeth Elliot and their missionary work to the previously unreached Auca tribe is a glowing testimony to an unyielding commitment to the gospel of Christ. That God's love and grace can be experienced in the midst of darkest tragedy is the ringing theme of this best of modern missionary stories.

Alexander Solzhenitsyn

One Day in the Life of Ivan Denisovich
The First Circle
Cancer Ward
The Gulag Archipelago
Nobel Lecture

Solzhenitsyn's own life is a paradigm of moral courage. He follows in the great Russian tradition of Tolstoy and Dostoevski in using his writing to explore humanity in the most extreme of situations. The twin capacity of human beings for both unspeakable cruelty and unbelievable courage is explored in his brilliant novels. Usually, it is faith in God which gives his characters the ability to carry on in the worst of circumstances. As a writer and as a man,

Solzhenitsyn stands in an exalted position among modern writers.

——————————————— ◆◆◆ ———————————————

If only there were evil people somewhere insidiously committing evil deeds and it were necessary only to separate them from the rest of us and destroy them. But the line dividing good and evil cuts through the heart of every human being. And who is willing to destroy a piece of his own heart?

—Alexander Solzhenitsyn, *The Gulag Archipelago*

——————————————— ◆◆◆ ———————————————

Frederick Buechner

The Book of Bebb
Telling the Truth
Godric

A brilliant sense of humor, and the aptitude to see the divine at work in the mundane circumstances of daily life, give Buechner's fiction and nonfiction an ability not only to move readers deeply, but also to help them see more deeply into their own lives. This sensitivity, wedded with an unflinching honesty about all of our doubts and questions concerning the life of faith, lifts his work above the propagandistic approach of so much religious writing. It is hard to pick the best of his work, for he maintains a high degree of quality throughout. *Telling the Truth: the Gospel as Tragedy, Comedy and Fairy Tale* demonstrates his ability as an essayist. The four Bebb novels (about a religious con man—or is he?)

and the artful retelling of the life of a medieval saint (*Godric*) show Buechner to be among our best modern novelists.

— ♦ ♦ ♦ —

"Praise, praise!" I croak. Praise God for all that's holy, cold, and dark. Praise him for all we lose, for all the river of years bears off. Praise him for stillness in the wake of pain. Praise him for emptiness. And as you race to spill into the sea, praise him yourself, old Wear. Praise him for dying and the peace of death.

In the little church I built of wood for Mary, I hollowed out a place for him. Perkin brings him by the pail and pours him in. Now that I can hardly walk, I crawl to meet him there. He takes me in his chilly lap to wash me of my sins. Or I kneel down beside him till within his depths I see a star.

Sometimes this star is still. Sometimes she dances. She is Mary's star. Within that little pool of Wear she winks at me. I wink at her. The secret that we share I cannot tell in full. But this much I will tell. What's lost is nothing to what's found, and all the death that ever was, set next to life, would scarcely fill a cup.

—Frederick Buechner, *Godric*

— ♦ ♦ ♦ —

Walter Wangerin

The Book of the Dun Cow
Ragman and Other Cries of Faith

An ordained Lutheran minister who once served an inner-city black congregation where he and his family were the only white members, Wangerin taught at a seminary before dedicating himself to write full-time. He now finds his congregation among those who eagerly await each new book. Wangerin's ability to craft one beautiful sentence after another and to deeply move the reader without becoming mawkish or sentimental make his books a rare and very enjoyable reading experience.

The Book of the Dun Cow is an award-winning fantasy which takes place in a barnyard. Its somber sequel, *The Book of Sorrows,* is equally powerful. *Ragman and Other Cries of Faith* is a collection of short stories, poems, and meditations that perhaps showcase Wangerin's talent at its best.

Shusaku Endo

The Silence

Writing as a Christian in a culture where Christianity is a very small minority (Japan), Endo has received wide acclaim from Christians and non-Christians alike for his gripping tales about the struggle of faith in an unbelieving world. *The Silence* is a harrowing tale about the persecution of Christians in old Japan. Without romanticizing, he shows the heroism of true commitment in the laying down of our lives (and our reputations) for our brothers and sisters.

Os Guinness

The Dust of Death
The American Hour

A student of Francis Schaeffer, Guinness has carried forward and deepened the former's cultural critique. Written in

1973, *The Dust of Death* is a prophetically insightful critique of both the good and the bad which the sixties bequeathed to us. His analysis is probing and foresaw many of the ruin-strewn paths down which our society has strayed. A more recent book, *The American Hour,* addresses the place of politics and society in the redemptive plan of God. This book is marked by levelheadedness, bold insight, the avoidance of extreme and simplistic formulas, and a willingness to critique all sides of the current struggle. To be both fair and God-honoring should be the goal of every critique; Guinness is a model of such in practice.

Henri Nouwen

The Way of the Heart
Genesee Diary

One of the premier modern writers about the spiritual life, Nouwen is a Catholic whose work touches those from all denominational and confessional groups due to its evocation of simple and honest devotion.

The Way of the Heart, a series of devotional meditations on the lives of the Desert Fathers, emphasizes the need to make solitude and inner silence a part of our spiritual maturation. *Genesee Diary* records Nouwen's experiences as he lives for an extended period of time with the monks in the Genesee monastery. It provides an honest and inspiring view of the life of the cloister.

The continuing body of work by Nouwen is one of this century's most nourishing spiritual treasures.

Hans Küng

On Being a Christian
Does God Exist?

Although it can be argued that Küng gives too much ground to modernism in his attempt to make Christianity relevant to the modern world, his writing is an example of that rarest of creatures: a top-notch scholar who is able to write books that are clear, entertaining, and relevant. His long-term battle against the doctrine of papal infallibility has earned him a censure from the Vatican, but he remains among the most influential of modern Catholic theologians. Even the reader whose theology is more conservative will find his books packed with acute insights and a deep historical understanding. In my estimation, *Does God Exist?* is one of the most impressive works of modern religious philosophy, and a stunning work of apologetics.

Annie Dillard

A Pilgrim at Tinker Creek
Teaching a Stone to Talk
The Writing Life

Dillard writes prose that is as dense and beautiful as poetry. Her books are full of achingly beautiful writing that reflects on the ways of God as evidenced in nature. She is an observer as acute as Thoreau, but with an underlying commitment to God's superintendence over the natural order. She is a mystic whose words take wing and soar; our hearts and minds cannot help but follow.

--- ◆ ◆ ◆ ---

It is difficult to undo our own damage, and to recall
to our presence that which we have asked to leave.
It is hard to desecrate a grove and change your
mind. The very holy mountains are keeping mum.
We doused the burning bush and cannot rekindle it;
we are lighting matches in vain under every green
tree.

What have we been doing all these centuries but
trying to call God back to the mountain, or, failing
that, raise a peep out of anything that isn't us? What
is the difference between a cathedral and a physics
lab? Are they not both saying: Hello!

—Annie Dillard, *A Pilgrim at Tinker Creek*

--- ◆ ◆ ◆ ---

Will Campbell

Brother to a Dragonfly

The autobiography of an early civil rights leader in the
Deep South. By turns this book is uproariously funny in its
salty language and down-home humor, and piercingly
prophetic. His definition of *grace*—"we're all bastards, but God
loves us anyway"—mirrors Campbell's courageous stand for
the dignity of all God's children and serves as a reminder of
how easy it is for the church to ride the wave of culture and
fail to take a stand on important issues of justice. Will
Campbell shows us that to be a Christian is to be fully human
and to be committed to respecting the humanity of all people.

Gustavo Gutierrez

A Theology of Liberation

As the seminal work of the liberation theology movement, this book emphasizes God's identification with the downtrodden and oppressed and calls the church to take a stand on the side of justice. Guiterrez's tone is more circumspect than some later works of liberation theology which emphasize the "necessity" of violence and a deep-seated hatred for the West. This movement is currently very influential, and this is a good book for grasping its ideas at their clearest and most sane.

Madeleine L'Engle

The Time Tetralogy
A Circle of Quiet

The Time Tetralogy, which begins with the award-winning *A Wrinkle in Time,* subtly explores theological issues in the guise of science fiction. While not as straightforward as the *Chronicles of Narnia* (and perhaps not as strictly orthodox either), these and other books by L'Engle give evidence of an alive and vibrant faith and a very personal vision. Unfortunately, her theology is at times suspect (showing influence from New Age sources), but the discerning reader will enjoy her memorable characters, vivid descriptions, and celebration of family life. The titles in the series include: *A Wrinkle in Time, A Wind in the Door, A Swiftly Tilting Planet,* and *Many Waters.*

A Circle of Quiet is the first in a series of journals which reflect on the events of her life, the surprising motions of grace, and the mystery of love and creativity. Also don't miss her strikingly original book on the relationship between faith and art, *Walking on Water.*

Vladimir Lossky

Mystical Theology of the Eastern Church

The third wing of the Christian church, the Orthodox tradition, is little known to most modern believers. Although possessing a long and rich tradition which arose out of its own set of historical circumstances, many people today would pause and scratch their heads at its mention. To get a flavor for this tradition as it has developed into the twentieth century, there is probably no better representative than Vladimir Lossky.

A much-respected modern work, *Mystical Theology of the Eastern Church* reflects the fact that the Orthodox tradition has never made a hard-and-fast distinction between theology and mysticism. Lossky's is a theology that gives a place of prominence to the role of the Holy Spirit in the believer's life. While most Protestants and Catholics may find much to disagree with here, it is nonetheless a very provocative and spiritually rich book.

Paul Johnson

Modern Times

Upon its publication, this book by historian Paul Johnson was embraced as an instant classic. It presents a uniquely conservative approach to understanding modern history. Johnson's style is witty, anecdotal, and immensely readable, but this does not compromise his thorough and careful historical analysis. This is not the kind of "dry-as-dust" chronicling of events that many have come to identify with history. Instead, it is history in the grand tradition: wide in scope, relevant, and intellectually penetrating.

Christian readers will applaud Johnson's contention that the blame for our modern malaise lies squarely on the shoulders of the rise of moral relativism. Many of Johnson's interpretations are reflective of his own conservative and Christian commitments.

If you wish to read just one book to help you understand our modern times, you could not do better than Johnson's entertaining and incisive analysis.

Charles Colson

Born Again
Kingdoms in Conflict
The Body

A former White House presidential advisor (under Richard Nixon), Colson served time in prison for his role in the Watergate scandal. He became a Christian just shortly before he was convicted, and strengthened his faith while in prison. After his release, he returned to prison, this time to minister to the needs of imprisoned convicts. His ministry, Prison Fellowship, has changed the lives of countless men and women. *Born Again* tells his story, and is one of the most convincing conversion stories of the twentieth century. *Kingdoms in Conflict* stakes out a balanced position on Christian involvement in politics, and *The Body* reminds the church of its mission in the modern world. Colson's books are filled with engaging historical stories, penetrating insights, and an unflagging commitment to presenting the gospel to modern men and women.

Peter J. Kreeft

Heaven: the Heart's Deepest Longing

Peter Kreeft is a philosophy professor with a unique knack for making even the most complex philosophical and theological ideas accessible to the common reader. The biggest influence on Kreeft seems to be C. S. Lewis, on whose work he has penned three books. This influence shows clearly in Kreeft's wonderful mix of intellectual and intuitive argumentation. His apologetical emphasis is certainly welcome in our confusing modern times, and he is a popularizer of the highest order. *Heaven: the Heart's Deepest Longing* uses Lewis's argument about longing as the basis for a marvelous study of heaven as the place all our hearts long for

Sheldon Vanauken

A Severe Mercy

In a true-life love story that is at once deeply romantic and spiritually uplifting, Vanauken relates the story of his own marriage to his wife, Davy. It is intoxicatingly romantic and, ultimately, deeply tragic. They built a love like few you will ever read of, only to have it torn from them by her early death of an incurable illness. Readers will find themselves challenged to deepen their own marriages, but warned against the danger of letting such relationships come between them and God. Readers will also find themselves challenged to live the life that God has given them with expectancy and wonder, cherishing every precious moment.

Richard Foster

The Celebration of Discipline
Prayer: the Heart's True Home

I have talked to many people who would concur with me, based on their own experience, that *Celebration of Discipline* is literally a life-changing book. In this book, Foster discusses the necessity for discipline in the Christian life through the practice of prayer, meditation, fasting, worship, service, and other spiritual disciplines. For me, the book opened up a whole new appreciation for the classics on spirituality and added depth and focus to my spiritual life. It is a book rich in practical insights and immensely challenging. Foster's book on prayer is equally powerful and one of the rare books on the subject which really does drive you joyfully to your knees.

— ◆◆◆ —

Superficiality is the curse of our age. The doctrine of instant satisfaction is a primary spiritual problem. The desperate need today is not for a greater number of intelligent people, or gifted people, but for deep people.

The classical disciplines of the spiritual life call us to move beyond surface living into the depths. They invite us to explore the inner caverns of the spiritual realm. They urge us to be the answer to a hollow world. . . .

Psalm 42:7 reads "Deep calls to deep." Perhaps somewhere in the subterranean chambers of your life you have heard the call to deeper, fuller living. You have become weary of frothy experiences and shallow teaching. Every now and then you have caught glimpses, hints of something more than you have known. Inwardly you long to launch out into the deep.

—Richard Foster, *The Celebration of Discipline*

———————————— ♦ ♦ ♦ ————————————

Dallas Willard

The Spirit of the Disciplines

An essential companion to Foster's books written by one of his close friends. A philosopher and theologian, Willard gives a biblical and theological justification for the centrality of the spiritual disciplines in the life of the growing believer. This is a profound look at the methods God uses to change our lives. Salvation, asserts Willard, is not only forgiveness of sins, but also transformation. A true must-read.

Susan Howatch

Glittering Images
Glamorous Powers

Howatch's series of novels about the clergy in the fictional English village of Starbridge are not without their faults: The plot and dialogue sometimes become a bit over-wrought, and some of the psychologizing is a bit much. These faults aside, however, Howatch has managed to accomplish something significant and important in these novels. She has produced a realistic and engrossing glimpse into the struggle of faith in our modern world. Her characters are not saints in the medieval sense of the word. They struggle against the temptations of the flesh: power, status, and especially, sex. Along the way we gain rich insights into the importance of facing the reality of our own hidden sin if we are to exult in the miracle of grace and forgiveness. These are the sort of books you could give to a nonbeliever to open up rich channels of discussion and witness. In addition to the two listed above, the series continues with *Ultimate Prizes, Scandalous Risks, Mystical Paths,* and *Absolute Truths.*

4

Why Read Non-Christian Books?

A book is like a garden carried in the pocket.

—CHINESE PROVERB

A book must be an ice-axe to break the seas frozen in our souls.

—FRANZ KAFKA

All that Mankind has done, thought, gained or been: it is lying as in magic preservation in the pages of books. They are the chosen possession of man.

—THOMAS CARLYLE

To suggest, as I have in previous chapters, that reading classic Christian books is a valuable and worthwhile undertaking will likely not be argued by many people. When, however, I suggest that it is also valuable to read the great writings of unbelievers, even of those hostile to Christianity, some will likely raise an eyebrow or protest that I am mistaken.

I follow the list of "Great Books of the Christian Tradition" with another list in Chapter 5: "Other Books Which Have Shaped Our World." We live in confusing and challenging times. Certain facets of Christian belief which formerly were widely accepted and unquestioned are now being dismissed by many in our culture. The very concept of truth itself is under vigorous attack.

Needless to say, this has given birth to an attitude of defensiveness among many believers who label all but the explicitly Christian as "dangerous" or unworthy of the attention of the faithful. Hence the writings of some of the greatest minds of all time, and the insights of some of our most penetrating modern thinkers, are dismissed from consideration by believers. The sad result of our good intentions is that we close ourselves off from one of the avenues through which God might teach us.

As modern evangelical Christians, we have created our own subculture. We have Christian music, Christian bookstores, Christian television, Christian schools, and just about anything else you might think of. There are some good things about this, but we face the grave danger of devaluing all that which does not specifically wear the label "Christian." When we separate ourselves to this extent, we lose our impact upon the culture at large and rob ourselves of the insights we could draw from those whose faith or worldview is different than ours.

Two Types of Revelation

There is a false form of spirituality which draws a sharp distinction between the earthly and heavenly spheres and dismisses the things of earth as unimportant. This is not biblical Christianity, but rather a form of Gnosticism or Neoplatonism. Biblical faith values the created order and believes that God is working out His purposes within the earthly sphere. When God became man in the person of Jesus Christ, His act forever sanctified what it means to be human. And so the human, earthly sphere of existence is never to be dismissed or taken lightly. Let us not try to be more spiritual than God Himself.

Theologians differentiate between two types of revelation, and it is here, perhaps, that the misunderstandings lie. The first is general revelation and is available to all people everywhere. The glories of nature, the innate moral law within us, and the logic of the created order are all sources that reveal something of God to us. These same sources are the basis for understanding God's created world. The second form of revelation is special revelation. Its primary focus is the revelation of God in the person of Jesus Christ, but it also includes the inspired record of God's dealings with His people, the Bible. Thomas Aquinas called these two forms of revelation "God's two books."

As believers we give a definite priority to special revelation, especially where it instructs us about the things of God. Where general revelation is often vague and cloudy (note the plethora of confusion in man-made religions based on general revelation), the special revelation of Scripture is quite clear in the essential elements of man's redemption and relationship with God. Therefore, we must focus our attention *primarily* on the Scriptures if we desire to be instructed in theology and personal holiness.

When we turn to matters of science, history, and medicine, it is not such a simple matter. Here we must be struck by the limitations of special revelation. Though it does indeed make some statements about these areas (and when it does, we must listen attentively), it does not speak exhaustively of them. It speaks truly, but not exhaustively. This means that we must turn to the data of general revelation to complete our knowledge. For example, the Bible is quite clear that God is the creator of the cosmos, but we are given few details on how it was done. Likewise, the Bible says nothing about the intricacies of quantum physics, medical science, botany, or geology. This should not be interpreted as a shortcoming in the Bible; it is just that the dispensing of this kind of information is not its purpose.

God has "written" another book to provide us with this kind of information: general revelation. When the Bible speaks, we must heed its authoritative words. When it is silent, we are called to use our God-given faculties of reason and creativity to experiment, inquire, and explore the book of nature. Because the two "books" have the same Author, when they both speak on a topic, they will ultimately never contradict each other. If we think we see a contradiction, it is only apparent. Either 1) we have misunderstood Scripture, not properly interpreting its meaning, or 2) we have misunderstood the facts of creation and have given them an incorrect interpretation. The facts of science and Scripture will never conflict. Only our false interpretations of one or the other will cause an apparent disagreement.

The Biblical Teaching on General Revelation

The Bible indicates that we can learn a great deal if we attend carefully to the world God created. Psalm 19 points to two different sources that can instruct us in the power and majesty of God: the book of nature (verses 1–6), and the book of the law (verses 7–14). Both Scripture and the created order speak to us of God's character:

The heavens declare the glory of God; the skies proclaim the work of his hands.
Day after day they pour forth speech; night after night they display knowledge.
There is no speech or language where their voice is not heard.
Their voice goes out into all the earth, their words to the ends of the world (Psalm 19:1–4).

If we train ourselves to attentiveness, having "ears to hear," nature itself can speak to us of the truth. Romans 1:18-32 offers a similar acknowledgment of nature's revelation: "For since the creation of the world God's invisible qualities—his eternal power and divine nature—have been clearly seen, being understood from what has been made, so that men are without excuse" (verse 20). Of course, as Paul points out, this knowledge has most often been ignored or perverted by sinful human beings. This is why we need the special revelation of God in Christ and the Word of God; the knowledge we gain from general revelation is not enough to save us, only enough to make us realize our predicament.

We can see this worked out in Paul's life and ministry. There are at least two clear instances in which Paul appealed to knowledge outside special revelation. In Acts 14:15–17, Paul and Barnabas were preaching in Lystra. When the people of the city mistook Paul and Barnabas for gods and wanted to sacrifice to them, Paul rebuked them, assuring them that he and Barnabas were not gods. However, Paul points out that they have no excuse for ignorance of the living God for "He has not left himself without testimony" (14:17). Here Paul was speaking not to Jews but to Greeks. He indicated that they could have some knowledge of the true God even though they had not been recipients of special revelation.

In Acts 17:22–31, Paul was preaching to the Greeks again, this time in Athens. When he saw that they had constructed an altar to "an Unknown God," he used it as an opportunity to draw a connection between what they knew and the good news of the gospel. The God that they had not known is the God whom Paul reveals to them. In making his case, Paul does something interesting, something important to the point of this chapter: In verse 28, he quotes one of their own pagan poets as a familiar and accurate source of information. Paul was not afraid to use secular sources when those sources spoke the truth. Paul could do this because he was committed to the idea that all truth is God's truth. There is no such thing as "Christian truth" as opposed to "non-Christian" truth.

General Revelation in the Christian Tradition

Because all truth is God's truth, the early Christian theologian Justin Martyr could write, "Whatever has been well said anywhere or by anyone belongs to us Christians" (*Apology* II, 13). This is not an attitude of arrogance, but of gratitude—gratitude for all the truth of God and His creation: the truths of science, art, sociology, psychology, as well as the truth of faith. Throughout Christian history, great thinkers have pointed to the fact that all knowledge is the province of the believer, that we have nothing to fear and everything to gain from the pursuit of truth wherever it is found. We must, as Augustine writes, mine the riches out of the secular culture:

> All branches of human learning have not only false
> and superstitious fancies . . . but they contain also
> liberal instruction which is better adapted to the use
> of truth, and some most excellent precepts of moral-
> ity; and some truths in regard even to the worship of
> the one God are found among them. Now these are,
> so to speak, their gold and silver, which they did not

create themselves, but dug out of the mines of God's providence which are everywhere scattered abroad.[1]

John Calvin manifested a similar attitude:

> Whenever, therefore, we meet with heathen writers, let us learn from that light of truth which is admirably displayed in their works, that the human mind, fallen as it is, and corrupted from its integrity, is yet invested and adorned by God with excellent talents. If we believe that the Spirit of God is the only fountain of truth, we shall neither reject nor despise the truth itself, wherever it shall appear, unless we wish to insult the Spirit of God.[2]

Further, not only must we rejoice in what we can learn from secular sources, but we should not belittle the importance of making ourselves knowledgeable in fields other than that of faith. We must work to bring God's redemptive work to bear on every area of knowledge. As Francis Schaeffer wrote:

> We must consciously reject the Platonic element which has been added to Christianity. God made the whole man; the whole man is redeemed in Christ. And after we are Christians, the Lordship of Christ covers the whole man. That includes his so-called spiritual things and his intellectual, creative and cultural things; it includes his law, his sociology, and psychology; it includes every single part and portion of a man and his being.[3]

Can we learn the humility to avoid the attitude that as Christians we have a corner on the truth? Instead, let us be open to learning even from those with whom we violently disagree. This is more than charity and courtesy; it is wisdom.

Learning from Nonbelievers

As the Israelites came up out of bondage in Egypt, so the Christian must rise out of the limitations of the modern secular worldview. We have, as they did, found the promise of freedom. In our case, we can be free from the stifling effects of a view of the world that ignores the basic truths of God's existence, power and love, and our human sinfulness and self-deception. To grasp these truths radically changes the way we think and live. The Israelites did not leave Egypt without "spoiling" their captors. They brought with them whatever they could that was valuable, useful, and worthy. So, too, we must not neglect to make use of the truths we can find in so-called "secular" thought. Of course, there is no such thing as secular truth as opposed to Christian truth. There are only true and false ways of thinking. The true ways of thinking are those rooted in correct interpretations of one or both of God's two forms of revelation. We must see that we can learn much from our "Egyptian" captors!

Christian values and ideas have influenced our culture so deeply that even unbelievers hold to remnants of truth. That is one of the reasons why we stand to learn much from non-Christians. Perhaps this situation is in the process of changing. The Christian worldview is less and less acceptable to many moderns; hence, the common ground is shrinking. But with all the necessary cautions, it is still true that most of our moral foundations, institutions, and attitudes are based upon Christian principles. The last couple of centuries may have distorted them, but the Christian influence in our culture is far from extinguished.

Another reason we can learn from unbelievers is that Christianity is about truth and reality. Believers and unbelievers share the same reality. When authors write about reality they cannot escape the deep truths about human nature and man's sinfulness. Many great novelists and philosophers have written about man's fallenness without ever using that phraseology.

We must have enough compassion to learn the questions of our time. Each age asks different questions about human identity, meaning, and purpose. The best of our modern novelists are articulating these questions. By reading them we find a window into the mental, emotional, and spiritual struggles of our own time. We cannot afford to be ignorant of how our contemporaries think if we are to make the good news of the gospel clear to them. Where they may have no answers for the questions they pose, we can point them to the answers which are found in the purposes of God.

We must also truly understand our opponents in the battle for men's hearts and minds. There are many people who purport to give answers (that we know are patently false) to the basic human questions. To counteract their misleading teachings, we must clearly hear what they are saying and bring the instruments of Scripture and human reason to bear on these issues. Thus we need to be aware of their ideas as well as biblical teachings.

Let us as believers remember when we become arrogant, thinking that we have a corner on the truth, that God used the Assyrians as a tool to correct Israel. These idol-worshipers were God's instrument to shape His people. If we are open enough today, He uses modern thinkers to correct the church. Though most of us would have serious disagreements with the likes of Marx, Sartre, and Nietzsche, they have some powerful words of correction that the church would do well to hear: words about authenticity, pharisaism, justice, and our current ineffectuality. Gregory, an early church father, suggests that we use secular culture as the Israelites did when they went to the Philistines to have their knives sharpened. We must learn to read dialectically, engaging in a conversation with the author, questioning, challenging, as well as learning.

The best of our Western culture is a storehouse for the best sub-Christian values. While these values may not be the whole story, they are nonetheless important for our society. These are values of the soul, not the spirit. They will not bring redemption, but then again, God created the soul as well as the spirit.

We have a phrase in English, "giving the devil his due," which seems to have originated in Shakespeare's *Henry IV, part 1. The Oxford English Dictionary* defines the meaning of this phrase as "to do justice even to a person of admittedly bad character or repute (or one disliked by the speaker)." We need humility, fairness, and objectivity to admit the truth, from whatever source it may come.

One final important point must be made. In order to navigate through the complexity and confusion of modern thought, we must have a thorough understanding of the Christian worldview. We must be intimately acquainted with the Scriptures if we are to withstand the onslaught of false teaching that comes to us along with the good insights. We can use the Bible as a plumb line against which modern deviations are measured and thereby avoided. Obviously, this is a hard and demanding call: to know the riches of Scripture and our Christian tradition while, at the same time, taking the time to know and understand our culture and its ideas. But it is a call to truly Christian thinking. If we can capture this vision, we can make a mark on our culture for Christ by bringing our perspectives to the table in any discussion with humility, creativity, and boldness. Let us open our minds to read widely and wisely. This discerning openness is a force that can not only transform our world, but also transform us.

5

Other Books Which Have Shaped Our World

How many a man has dated a new era in his life from the reading of a book!

—HENRY DAVID THOREAU

Books are the compass and telescopes and sextants and charts which other men have prepared to help us navigate the dangerous seas of human life.

—JESSE LEE BENNETT

Books are the carriers of civilization. Without books, history is silent, literature dumb, science crippled, thought and speculation at a standstill. Without books, the development of civilization would have been impossible. They are engines of change, windows on the world, "lighthouses" (as a poet said) "erected in the sea of time." They are companions, teachers, magicians, bankers of the treasures of the mind. Books are humanity in print.

—BARBARA TUCHMAN

The Ancient World

It is to our own detriment that modern Christians are, in general, unfamiliar with the great classics of Greece and Rome. It is clear that the apostle Paul was an attentive student of these books and used them to aid in the proclamation of the gospel (see Acts 17:28). The ancient writers were close observers of humanity who help us better understand ourselves and the need for human beings to live ethically and with dignity.

◆◆◆

Homer (c. 850 B.C.)

The Iliad
The Odyssey

How can you overpraise Homer, the fountainhead of Western literature? When read in a good translation (like Richmond Lattimore's *The Iliad* and Robert Fitzgerald's *The Odyssey*), these are works of intense beauty and riveting action, full of memorable incidents and characters and truly heroic (if flawed) examples of virtue and character.

──────────────── ♦ ♦ ♦ ────────────────

Sing in me, Muse, and through me tell the story
of that man skilled in all ways of contending,
the wanderer, harried for years on end,
after he plundered the stronghold
on the proud height of Troy.

—Homer, *The Odyssey*

──────────────── ♦ ♦ ♦ ────────────────

Aeschylus (525–456 B.C.)

The Orestia
Prometheus Bound

The Orestia is a difficult but powerful trilogy of plays about revenge, guilt, and atonement from the first of the great Greek dramatists. I recommend the translation by Richmond Lattimore. *Prometheus Bound* is a mythic drama on human limitation in the face of the power of the gods.

Sophocles (c. 496–406 B.C.)

Oedipus the King
Antigone
Philoctetes

Oedipus is, of course, the archetypical Greek play, and dramatists, novelists, philosophers, and psychologists have all explored its rich and evocative themes. It is a truly great work, but the other plays by Sophocles are also worth attention.

Aristophanes (c. 448–380 B.C.)

The Clouds
The Frogs
The Birds
Lysistrata

The witty and bawdy humor of Aristophanes still holds up well after all these centuries. The targets of his wit remain current: philosophy and the academic life (*The Clouds*), literature and drama (*The Frogs*), sex and male/female relationships (*Lysistrata*), and politics (*The Birds*). His comedies are at the same time vulgar and lyrical. One must read him to see how this is possible.

Euripides (c. 484–406 B.C.)

Trojan Women
The Bacchae

The last of the great Athenian dramatists, Euripides's work is marked by its cynicism. In this and other ways he is much closer to the modern temper than the older Greek dramatists.

Plato (c. 428–348 B.C.)

The Symposium
The Republic
Last Dialogues of Socrates

One modern philosopher has written that all the history of philosophy is merely a footnote to Plato. The measure of

Plato's greatness is that this is hardly an overstatement. The profundity of his work has left an indelible mark on the way we live and think. Christian philosophers through the ages have found much in Plato to illuminate the human experience and our relationship to the divine. Most recently, the work of Eric Voegelin has used Plato's thought as a guide to the complexities of history and existence. For both depth of wisdom and pure entertainment (the dialogues are both utterly convincing and sometimes wryly humorous), the work of Plato deserves close reading by Christians.

———————————— ♦♦♦ ————————————

Until philosophers are kings, or the kings and princes of the world have the spirit and power of philosophy, and political greatness and wisdom meet in one, and those commoner natures who pursue either to the exclusion of the other are compelled to stand aside, cities will never have rest from their evils—no, nor the human race, as I believe—and then only will this our State have a possibility of life and behold the light of day.

—Plato, *The Republic*

———————————— ♦♦♦ ————————————

Aristotle (384–322 B.C.)

Nicomachean Ethics
Poetics

For the sheer magnitude of the subjects that Aristotle (Plato's student and teacher of Alexander the Great) covered in his many writings, there is no comparison. His knowledge was encyclopedic, and his logic was careful and usually persuasive. Aristotle set the terms for most of the ongoing theological and philosophical disputes that raged from the Middle Ages on, making him, along with Plato, the twin pillars upon which Western thought is founded. A valuable introduction for the beginning reader of Aristotle is Mortimer J. Adler's *Aristotle for Everybody.*

———————————————— ♦ ♦ ♦ ————————————————

For the man who flies from and fears everything and does not stand his ground against anything becomes a coward, and the man who fears nothing at all but goes to meet every danger becomes rash; and similarly the man who indulges in every pleasure and abstains from none becomes self-indulgent, while the man who shuns every pleasure, as boors do, becomes in a way insensible; temperance and courage, then are destroyed by excess and defect, and preserved by the mean.

—Aristotle, *Nicomachean Ethics*

———————————————— ♦ ♦ ♦ ————————————————

Lucretius (c. 95–55 B.C.)

On the Nature of Things

This poetic philosophical musing by the first great materialist philosopher, and an early Western proponent of atheism, anticipated many of the prejudices of modern secularism centuries before their rise.

Virgil (70–19 B.C.)

The Aeneid

Virgil's epic can only be matched by the work of Homer, his great model. This powerful poem deals with events following the fall of Troy and the founding of the Roman empire. A stately and often tragic work, the translation by Robert Fitzgerald is particularly good.

Marcus Aurelius (121–180)

Meditations

A Roman emperor and stoic philosopher, Aurelius meditates on the vicissitudes of human existence and on how to live in peace and serenity in the midst of a chaotic world. A work of beauty and depth.

––––––––––––––– ♦♦♦ –––––––––––––––

Let thy chief fort and place of defense be, a mind free from passions. A stronger place and better fortified than this, hath no man.

—Marcus Aurelius, *Meditations*

––––––––––––––– ♦♦♦ –––––––––––––––

Plotinus (205–270)

Enneads

Highly influential to the mystical tradition, Plotinus takes the Platonic theories a step further in his teachings, emphasizing the release of the soul from the prison of the body. Some extreme forms of medieval mysticism unfortunately tried to incorporate these ideas into Christianity and produced a form of faith that deprecates the human experience and the joy of the created order.

The Middle Ages

*T*he Middle Ages most definitely show the stamp of a predominantly Christian culture. This was a time when just about everything revolved around the Christian vision of reality (even though it was sometimes rather imperfectly lived out). Even those writers listed here were operating at the fringes of the Christian worldview. But changes were brewing that would eventually bring secularism into ascendancy.

Snorri Sturluson (1179–1241)

Prose Edda

This is the classic source for much of Norse mythology: Odin, Thor, the battles of the gods and the final apocalyptic war, Ragnarok. These tales of violence and valor have provided the themes for a great deal of European culture. Christians will find it interesting to note how Sturluson, in the early chapters of this work, attempts to connect this mythology with biblical stories.

Unknown

Beowulf

A heroic narrative poem from the early Anglo-Saxon tradition about the battle of Beowulf against a dragon. Many astute readers will note the undoubtedly purposeful but subtle analogies to the Gospels.

Petrarch (1304–1374)

Sonnets

Ascent of Mt. Ventoux

This author of romantic lyrical love poems, and a key figure in our modern conception of romance, was one of the founders of Renaissance humanism. His *Ascent of Mt. Ventoux* in some ways parallels Augustine's *Confessions,* providing an interesting comparison to the conversion of Augustine, as a similar experience nets very different results.

Giovanni Boccaccio (1313–1375)

The Decameron

A collection of tales about love, romance, sex, unfaithfulness, and deception. Frequently uproariously funny, often in bad taste, nearly always entertaining.

The Early
Modern World

The Renaissance was a rebirth of classical civilization, a revaluation of the dignity of the individual human being, and a new openness to intellectual inquiry. Breaking free of the bonds of tradition gave a new impulse to the arts and sciences, but it also planted the seeds of a new worldview, one which pushed God and religion toward the periphery of human knowledge. Some thinkers stressed human autonomy to such a degree that the importance of faith was greatly diminished.

Leonardo da Vinci (1452–1519)

Notebooks

These notebooks of one of the greatest painters show a man of incredible intelligence and creativity, and an inventor of astonishing fertility. It is to him that the phrase "Renaissance man" most fully refers.

Machiavelli (1469–1527)

The Prince

In this guide for those in places of leadership, Machiavelli shows the truth of the old motto: The more things change, the more they stay the same. His advice is mercenary and tyrannical, but from a historical perspective is frighteningly effective.

Rabelais (c. 1483–1553)

Gargantua and Pantagruel

A long, witty work which is a strange mixture of fantasy, satire, and bawdy humor. It is notable for its rich language and odd plot twists. By all means, try to locate the translation by Sir Thomas Urquart and Peter Motteux, which so well captures the marvelously playful way that Rabelais used words.

Michel de Montaigne (1533–1592)

Essays

One of the great prose stylists of all time, Montaigne's wise and witty essays range over almost every conceivable subject. He boldly puts forth himself, his own personality, as the main subject of his work. Montaigne strove to ask questions that penetrate beyond appearances and challenge our perceptions: "When I play with my cat who knows if she does not amuse herself more with me than I with her?" T. S. Eliot said of him that he gives voice to the skepticism in every human heart, and many credit him as one of the founders of relativism.

◆ ◆ ◆

Each man calls barbarism whatever is not his own practice; for indeed it seems we have no other test of truth than the example and pattern of the opinions and customs of the country we live in.

—Michel de Montaigne, *Essays*

◆ ◆ ◆

Miguel de Cervantes (1547–1616)

Don Quixote

A humorous, touching, and overlong novel of a knight errant and his adventures. Full of funny scenes and clever conversations, it is one of the few books which I would recommend reading in an abridgment.

Francis Bacon (1561–1626)

Essays
The New Atlantis

Thought-provoking essays and futuristic thinking by the early English philosopher who coined the phrase "knowledge is power."

Thomas Hobbes (1588–1679)

Leviathan

An English political philosopher whose religious skepticism was ahead of its time.

Rene Descartes (1596–1650)

Discourse On Method

This French philosopher, author of the famous "I think therefore I am," taught that certainty came from intuition and deduction, and emphasized the split between mind and matter. Pascal aimed much of his book *Pensees* at refuting Descartes's self-assured conclusions.

Molière (1622–1673)

The Imaginary Invalid
The Misanthrope
Tartuffe
The School for Wives

Hilarious dramas of social foibles which hold up well in our modern times. The clever dialogue, frenetic plot twists, and humorous characterizations make Moliere a delight to read. Richard Wilbur's excellent translations capture well the marvelous humor of this talented comic playwright.

Benedict de Spinoza (1632–1677)

Ethics

The major work of this Jewish pantheistic philosopher, marked by logical argumentation and tolerance.

John Locke (1632–1704)

Essay Concerning Human Understanding

One of the key modern works in philosophy, this essay focuses on the question of epistemology, "How can we know?" Locke was famous for the idea of the "tabula rasa" (the blank slate). Not an easy read, but full of influential ideas.

The Eighteenth Century

*T*he *Enlightenment was a time of the exchange of certainties. No longer was religion seen to have the undisputable answers to human questionings. Enlightenment thinkers instead saw reason as the final court of appeal in the quest for understanding. This period was one of great confidence in man's ability to solve humanity's problems and create a better world through use of reason. But the failure of many of these thinkers to fully reckon with the reality of human fallenness opened the door to the excesses and cruelties of the coming age of revolutions. The eventual decline of confidence in the power of reason left mankind searching but not finding.*

Voltaire (1694–1778)

Candide

Voltaire epitomizes the Enlightenment for many readers. His trust in reason seems unquenchable, but he also saw the foibles of human beings and their addiction to superstitions. His writing is lively, immensely enjoyable, and provides much food for thought, even if his thinking is not always satisfying. Parts of *Candide* will leave you laughing out loud.

———————————— ♦♦♦ ————————————

If God did not exist it would be necessary to invent Him.

Prejudices are what fools use for reason.

Man is not born wicked; he becomes so in the same way as he becomes sick.

Of all religions, Christianity is without doubt the one that should inspire tolerance most, although, up to now, the Christians have been the most intolerant of all men.

—Voltaire, various aphorisms

———————————— ♦ ♦ ♦ ————————————

Henry Fielding (1707–1754)

Tom Jones

A rowdy and ribald coming-of-age novel, full of incident and adventure.

David Hume (1711–1776)

An Enquiry Concerning Human Understanding

A British philosopher of empiricism, Hume's ideas have had a major effect on modern thinking.

Jean Jacques Rousseau (1712–1778)

Confessions
The Social Contract

To say that Rousseau, the great predecessor of the Romantics, was modern before his time is not necessarily to be complimentary, for he represents much that is unpleasant in modern beliefs and attitudes: an egotistical preoccupation with self, a disregard for authority and tradition, and an unrealistically utopian view of human nature. He is, however, a writer of clarity and interest.

——————————————— ♦ ♦ ♦ ———————————————

Man is born free, and everywhere he is in chains. . . .

By equality, we should understand, not that the degrees of power and riches are to be absolutely identical for everybody; but that power shall never be so strong as to be capable of violence and shall always be exercised by virtue of rank and law; and that, in respect to riches, no citizen shall ever be wealthy enough to buy another, and none poor enough to be forced to sell himself.

—Jean Jacques Rousseau, *The Social Contract*

——————————————— ♦ ♦ ♦ ———————————————

Laurence Sterne (1713–1768)

Tristram Shandy

In this strange and experimental novel, Sterne uses techniques that predate many of the moderns.

Adam Smith (1723–1790)

The Wealth of Nations

The classic defense of capitalism and the "hidden hand" that makes it function.

Immanuel Kant (1724–1804)

The Critique of Pure Reason

Extremely difficult philosophical exploration of the nature of human reason. Read about him in a good history of philosophy first. (I can recommend no better than Frederick Copleston's, now published in three lengthy paperback volumes.)

Thomas Paine (1737–1809)

The Rights of Man

An important document in the American call for independence, and a searing indictment of tyranny and injustice.

Edward Gibbon (1737–1794)

Decline and Fall of the Roman Empire

In Gibbon's famous study of the causes for the fall of the Roman empire, Christianity is criticized as one of the key factors. Most modern historians would dispute much of his argument, but it remains an influential work.

James Boswell (1740–1795)

The Life of Samuel Johnson

This biography of one of the greatest men of letters is full of insight, humor, and entertaining anecdote.

James Madison (1751–1836) and Others

The Federalist Papers

A collection of documents containing the debates on how to construct a truly free and just government. These are the ideas that created the American political structure.

The Nineteenth Century

*T*his was the century of "isms" (Positivism, Roman-
ticism, Marxism, etc.), a time of searching for some
system of thought that would make sense of life's realities. In
the wake of Christianity's decline in influence in the intellectual
sphere, men and women sought for answers in science, in
political and economic justice, in art, and in nature. The only
common element was their failure to provide a satisfying alter-
native to the Christian faith. Many of the issues which they
brought forward, however, must be grappled with by Christians
who wish to bring the lordship of Christ to bear on all life.

♦ ♦ ♦

Wolfgang von Goethe (1749–1832)

Faust
Sorrows of the Young Werther

As important to Germany as Shakespeare was to England,
Goethe excelled in almost every literary genre he attempted.
These studies of the temptation of knowledge (Faust) and
despair (Werther) are good places to start. Goethe was a
humanist who practiced the religion of the self and believed in
redemption through expanding one's own personality.

Georg Wilhelm Friedrich Hegel (1770–1831)

The Phenomenology of Spirit

Hegel's almost unreadable philosophical text contains
many interesting ideas. It is, however, difficult to sort them

out in the dense thicket of his writing style. This work, nonetheless, has had a profound influence on modern philosophy.

William Wordsworth (1770–1850)

Poems

This English Romantic poet with a love for nature and a concern for the spiritual life of mankind was influenced by a Platonic form of Christian thought. His magnificent poems are powerful, rich, and memorable.

◆ ◆ ◆

Our birth is but a sleep and a forgetting:
The Soul that rises with us, our life's Star,
    Hath had elsewhere its setting,
      And cometh from afar.
Not in entire forgetfulness,
And not in utter nakedness
But trailing clouds of glory do we come
    From God, who is our home:
Heaven lies about us in our infancy!
Shades of the prison-house begin to close
    Upon the growing Boy.

          —William Wordsworth, Ode:
          "Intimations of Immortality"

◆ ◆ ◆

Jane Austen (1775–1817)

Pride and Prejudice
Emma

Austen's novels of manners put forward high moral ideals, but never stoop to preachiness or sentimentalism. Austen seems to have a deep distrust of the kind of romantic love celebrated in our modern films and books.

Stendhal (1783–1842)

The Red and the Black

A thoroughly engaging novel about a young man who uses all means necessary to advance his own position in life. A well-drawn slice of life in eighteenth- and nineteenth-century France.

Lord Byron [George Gordon] (1788–1824)

Poems

Perhaps more known for his rakish lifestyle than for his poems, they are, nonetheless, worthy of attention.

Percy Bysshe Shelley (1792–1822)

Poems

Shelley's deeply felt atheism is one of the factors that make his poems original and memorable. He is one of the most intellectually challenging of the English Romantic poets.

John Keats (1795–1821)

Poems

A fine English poet from a century that produced several. Keats mixes a classical restraint with an interest in supernatural and spiritualistic themes.

Mary Shelley (1797–1851)

Frankenstein

A powerful novel and a cautionary tale about the egotistic ambitions of human beings who seek to play God. Not to be confused with the Frankenstein movies of the 1930s, this is a very serious and profound work.

Auguste Comte (1798–1857)

The Positive Philosophy

The archetypical work of one of the intellectual trends of the nineteenth century, Comte's work celebrates knowledge through science in positively religious terms. Comte captures the self-assured tone of those who see no need for God in the modern scientific world.

Honoré Balzac (1799–1850)

Pere Goirot

One of the better novels by this prolific French writer, *Pere Goirot* is full of wonderful character studies and well-drawn cultural background.

Victor Hugo (1802–1885)

Les Miserables

Long but powerful novel set in France. Worth the effort it takes to read, since it reveals both the pains and joys of existence. Javert's unflinching pursuit of the humble and repentant thief is a story of heroism, injustice, love, and the limits of revenge. This is one of those few novels that are better read in an abridgment, as Hugo has a tendency to wax eloquently and at length about matters peripheral to the story.

Ralph Waldo Emerson (1803–1882)

Essays and Sermons

An American philosopher and pundit of the transcendental school, Emerson has deeply influenced the popular American consciousness and affected the way many people think about religion and ethics.

––––––––––––––––– ♦♦♦ –––––––––––––––––

Whoso would be a man, must be a nonconformist. He who would gather immortal palms must not be hindered by the name of goodness, but must explore if it be goodness. Nothing is at last sacred but the integrity of your own mind. . . . A man is to carry himself in the presence of opposition as if every thing were titular and ephemeral but he. I am ashamed to think how easily we capitulate to badges and names, to large societies and dead institutions.

—Ralph Waldo Emerson, *On Self Reliance*

––––––––––––––––– ♦♦♦ –––––––––––––––––

Nathaniel Hawthorne (1804–1864)

The Scarlet Letter

A biased but emotionally stirring view of the Puritans through the eyes of one who had little sympathy for them. Themes of guilt and confession are powerfully portrayed in this novel.

Alexis de Tocqueville (1805–1873)

Democracy in America

This French writer traveled throughout America and recorded his thoughts and predictions concerning this then-young country. Astoundingly prophetic and sagely wise.

John Stuart Mill (1806–1873)

On Liberty
The Subjection of Women
Autobiography

Mill's call for tolerance and liberty is as relevant now as it was then. His writing style is felicitous and his exposition clear and thought-provoking. One of the greatest men of the nineteenth century.

— ♦ ♦ ♦ —

It is a piece of idle sentimentality that truth, merely as truth, has any inherent power denied to error or prevailing against the dungeon and the stake. Men are not more zealous for truth than they often are for error. . . . The real advantage which truth has consists in this, that when an opinion is true, it may be extinguished once, twice, or many times, but in the course of ages there will generally be found persons to rediscover it.

—John Stuart Mill, *On Liberty*

———————————— ♦ ♦ ♦ ————————————

Charles Darwin (1809–1882)

Origin of Species
The Descent of Man

These two works summarize the findings of Darwin and explain his theory of evolution. Darwin's critics should note the caution with which many of his ideas are expressed. This is at variance with may modern evolutionists who treat the theory as a proven fact. There are many shamelessly poor critiques of Darwin on the market. One that deserves attention for its accuracy, tone, and scientific respectability is Philip Johnson's *Darwin on Trial*.

Edgar Allan Poe (1809–1849)

Short Stories

Poe had a grasp of the diabolical and the horrible that somehow makes his strange tales very convincing. His style is so lyrical that even the most unthinkable events are cast in a strangely fascinating light.

Charles Dickens (1812–1870)

David Copperfield
The Pickwick Papers
Hard Times
A Christmas Carol
A Tale of Two Cities

Dickens could sometimes be faulted for being overlong and sentimental, but his novels seem to lodge in the memory long after they are read. His ability to create a multitude of memorable characters gave us the adjective "Dickensian." His staunch Victorian morality is a pleasant contrast to our modern sense of moral drift.

Charlotte Brontë (1816–1855)

Jane Eyre

The life of a virtuous and intelligent young woman is captured in this novel, which has one of the most satisfying love stories in literature. This wise book has much to teach us about the nature of real love.

Henry David Thoreau (1817–1862)

Walden
Civil Disobedience

Thoreau escaped to the world of nature and recorded his observations in his book *Walden*. What he learned encompasses not only nature itself, but also the purpose and conduct of human lives. This beautifully written book is a refreshing tonic for the modern city-dweller.

—————————————————————— ◆ ◆ ◆ ——————————————————————

I went to the woods because I wished to live deliber-
ately, to front only the essential facts of life, and see
if I could not learn what it had to teach, and not,
when I came to die, discover that I had not lived. . . .

I wanted to live deep and suck out all the marrow
of life, to live so sturdily and Spartan-like as to put to
rout all that was not life, to cut a broad swath and
shave close, to drive life into a corner, and reduce it
to its lowest terms, and, if it proved to be mean, why
then to get the whole and genuine meanness of it,
and publish its meanness to the world; or if it were
sublime, to know it by experience and be able to give
an account of it.

—Henry David Thoreau, *Walden*

—————————————————————— ◆ ◆ ◆ ——————————————————————

Emily Brontë (1818–1848)

Wuthering Heights

A haunting story of enduring love and vengeful hatred
that has gained a wide readership. An emotional exploration
of human nature and its limitations.

Ivan Turgenev (1818–1883)

Fathers and Sons

This novelistic treatment of the struggle between generations gave us the word *nihilistic,* a term for the philosophy

that life is utterly without meaning. Turgenev used it to capture the ideas of one of the main characters in this book.

Karl Marx (1818–1883)

Capital
The Communist Manifesto

Capital is an extremely difficult work of economics, but the *Manifesto* is probably the clearest way to get in touch with his major ideas. For Marx on religion, one might want to peruse his "Theses on Feuerbach." For a vitriolic criticism of Marx the man and thinker, see Paul Johnson's chapter on Marx in his book *Intellectuals*.

—————————— ♦ ♦ ♦ ——————————

The history of all hitherto existing society is the history of class struggles. . . .

The Communists disdain to conceal their views and aims. They openly declare that their ends can be attained only by the forcible overthrow of all existing social conditions. Let the ruling classes tremble at a Communist revolution. The proletarians have nothing to lose but their chains. They have a world to win.

Workingmen of all countries, unite!
—Karl Marx (with Frederich Engels),
The Communist Manifesto

—————————— ♦ ♦ ♦ ——————————

George Eliot (1819–1880)

Middlemarch

Writing under a male pseudonym, George Eliot (Mary Ann Evans) was one of the finest female novelists of the nineteenth century. Henry James said of her novels: "There rises from them a kind of fragrance of moral elevation; a love of justice, truth, and light; a large, generous way of looking at things; and a constant effort to hold high the torch in the dusky spaces of man's conscience." A well-constructed plot about the pain of lofty goals turned sour by poor choices.

Herman Melville (1819–1891)

Moby Dick
Billy Budd

Some parts of *Moby Dick* can be rather tedious, but when the story finally unravels itself, there is much potent symbolism and some hauntingly good writing. Though less well known, *Billy Budd,* a story about the trials of a Christlike sailor, is a stirring allegorical tale.

Walt Whitman (1819–1892)

Leaves of Grass

This collection of distinctly American poems was written and rewritten throughout Whitman's life. Concerned with self-analysis and self-development, Whitman's poetry predates many modern attitudes about the human soul and spirit.

Gustave Flaubert (1821–1880)

Madame Bovary

A gripping novel about the lure and destructiveness of adultery, written by a French writer of graceful style and penetrating insight.

Charles Baudelaire (1821–1867)

Les fleurs du mal (Flowers of Evil)

The poetry of this French writer is concerned largely with the dark and degraded side of human nature.

Henrik Ibsen (1828–1906)

A Doll's House
Hedda Gabler
The Master Builder
The Wild Duck

These gripping tragic dramas deal with the submerged feelings and passions of modern people. Ibsen was ahead of his time in the topicality of his subjects and is considered by many to be one of the finest playwrights of all time.

Emily Dickinson (1830–1886)

Poems

Short and highly subjective visions of life by a reclusive woman who saw deeply into nature, other people, and herself. Her poetry is highly intellectual and carefully wrought.

─────────────── ♦ ♦ ♦ ───────────────

My life closed twice before its close—
It yet remains to see
If immortality unveil
A third event for me
So huge, so hopeless to conceive
As these that twice befell.
Parting is all we know of heaven,
And all we need of hell.

—Emily Dickinson

─────────────── ♦ ♦ ♦ ───────────────

Lewis Carroll (1832–1898)

Alice in Wonderland

A masterpiece of children's literature written by a playful philosophy professor, this book works on many levels. There is more here than meets the eye.

Mark Twain (1835–1910)

Tom Sawyer
Huckleberry Finn

These roaringly funny and nostalgic novels are much more than merely boys' books. Full of beauty and insight into human nature, *Huckleberry Finn* is considered by many to be the greatest American novel. If you enjoy these, try the hilarious *Innocents Abroad*.

Henry Adams (1838–1919)

The Education of Henry Adams
Mont St. Michel and Chartres

A highly aesthetically driven American author longs for the good old days . . . the Middle Ages!

Thomas Hardy (1840–1928)

Far From the Madding Crowd
Tess of the D'Urbervilles

Tragic and deeply pessimistic, these ultimately powerful novels about the passions that lie just beneath the surface of the tranquil English country life reveal a potent vision of a moral universe without God.

William James (1842–1910)

Principles of Psychology
Varieties of Religious Experiences

The clearheadedness and pragmatism of James make him an informative and attractive philosopher. His book on religious experiences is fascinating and surprisingly sympathetic.

Henry James (1843–1919)

Portrait of a Lady
Turn of the Screw
Daisy Miller

An American novelist whose power is revealed in the restraint of his writing and his sure sense of observation.

Oscar Wilde (1854–1900)

The Importance of Being Earnest
Lady Windermere's Fan

The exceptionally witty plays by the notorious Oscar Wilde are among the finest comic gems in all of theater.

Friedrich Nietzsche (1844–1900)

Beyond Good and Evil
Thus Spake Zarathustra
The Genealogy of Morals

Nietzsche's analysis of what is wrong with the modern world is extremely perceptive, but his solutions will be unacceptable to most believers. I believe Nietzsche to be wrong in just about every conclusion he drew, but in such a highly literate way that he makes for important reading and provides an excellent foil for examining the weaknesses of our own ideas.

———————————— ♦♦♦ ————————————

"Whither is God?" he cried. "I shall tell you. We have killed him—you and I. All of us are his murderers. But how have we done this? How were we able to drink up the sea? Who gave us the sponge to wipe away the entire horizon? . . . Do we not feel the breath of empty space? Has it not become colder? Is not night and more night coming on all the time? Must not lanterns be lit in the morning? Do we not hear anything yet of the noise of the gravediggers who are burying God? Do we not smell anything yet of God's decomposition? Gods, too, decompose. God is dead. And we have killed him."

—Friedrich Nietzsche, *Thus Spake Zarathustra*

———————————— ♦♦♦ ————————————

Robert Louis Stevenson (1850–1894)

Dr. Jekyll and Mr. Hyde

This parable of the two sides of human nature and how they struggle within an individual's life makes an exciting and entertaining tale.

Sigmund Freud (1856–1939)

The Interpretation of Dreams
Introductory Lectures on Psychoanalysis
Civilization and Its Discontents

Even his most strident opponents must admit to the brilliance and creativity of Freud's work. Even if we disagree with some of his foundational ideas, we must be captured by his brave attempt to fathom the human psyche. As with other very original writers, much of his work is almost completely misunderstood in the popular conception. See Bruno Bettleheim's sympathetic book *Freud and Man's Soul* for a look at some of these misconceptions. The best critique of Freud which I have seen from a Chrisitan perspective is the valuable book by Paul C. Vitz, *Sigmund Freud's Christian Unconscious*.

——————————— ◆◆◆ ———————————

Sublimation of instinct is an especially conspicuous feature of cultural evolution; this it is that makes it possible for the higher mental operations, scientific, artistic, ideological activities, to play such an important part in civilized life. . . . It is impossible to ignore the extent to which civilization is built upon renunciation of instinctual gratifications, the degree to which the existence of civilization presupposes the non-gratification (suppression, repression or something else?) of powerful instinctual urgencies. This "cultural privation" dominates the whole field of social relations between human beings; we know already that it is the cause of the antagonism against which all civilization has to fight. . . .

The symptoms of neurosis, as we have learnt, are essentially a substitute for unfulfilled sexual wishes.

—Sigmund Freud, *Civilization and Its Discontents*

◆ ◆ ◆

Max Weber (1864–1920)

The Protestant Ethic and the Spirit of Capitalism

This ground-breaking sociological study of the Protestant ethic is surprisingly readable and very provocative. Even if you don't agree with his thesis (and many scholars do not), you must come to terms with it if you are interested in the questions of economics, work ethics, or the nature of capitalism.

Stephen Crane (1871–1900)

The Red Badge of Courage

A short novel which captures the horror of the American civil war as seen through the eyes of a young soldier who is alternately caught up in the excitement of battle and terrified by its ferocity.

The Twentieth Century

There is a pervasive note of despair that runs through much of the art, music, literature, and philosophy of modern times. In our relativistic age, many people have given up hope of finding any real answers to life's perplexing questions. This has tended to produce work that is intricate, witty, or complex on the exterior, but morally hollow at its core. We appear to be a culture that is dying, losing that which gave us the strength to achieve much of our greatness. But these despairing voices surrounding us do us a service in clearly pointing people to their need for the hope and meaning which is available in the gospel.

◆◆◆

George Bernard Shaw (1856–1950)

Man and Superman
Saint Joan
Arms and the Man
Major Barbara
Heartbreak House

Shaw had a unique gift for dramatizing the most critical moral and ethical issues in such a way that his plays are extremely insightful, as well as howlingly funny. His more serious philosophical thinking is usually undistinguished and unconvincing, yet so delightfully put forward that it cannot but capture one's attention.

Joseph Conrad (1857–1924)

The Heart of Darkness

Conrad's haunting vision of the darkness and savagery that lie just below the surface of human civilization makes this a very disturbing book.

John Dewey (1859–1952)

Democracy and Education

Dewey gives fascinating insights on the necessity of good education to make democracy work.

Anton Chekhov (1860–1904)

The Seagull
The Cherry Orchard

Two of many great plays by the Russian dramatist whose main focus was upon character development, rather than a concern for plot.

William Butler Yeats (1865–1939)

Poems

This great Irish poet was deeply influenced by myth, folklore, and various religious traditions. His poetry is full of unforgettable imagery. See especially his haunting vision of the modern world in his poem "The Second Coming."

Luigi Pirandello (1867–1936)

Five Characters in Search of an Author

A bizarre and stunningly original drama by an Italian great, which turns many of the conventions of drama on their heads.

Marcel Proust (1871–1922)

Remembrance of Things Past

Very lengthy and nostalgic novel about how the past lives on in the future. A major work that some people may find tedious at times. A work much praised but little read by anybody except students of French literature.

Robert Frost (1874–1963)

Poems

A major American poet whose work is accessible and heartfelt. He was one of those rarest of modern phenomena: a great poet who was appreciated by a wide audience.

Carl Jung (1875–1961)

Modern Man in Search of a Soul

The great psychologist meditates in this book on the human need for spiritual sustenance in life. Jung's diagnosis is brilliant, though I find his answers to be less than satisfactory. His many contributions to modern psychological thought can be glimpsed in the short guide by Calvin S. Hall and Vernon J. Nordby, *A Primer of Jungian Psychology*. It is troubling that most of Jung's later work veered toward rather occultic themes.

Rainer Maria Rilke (1875–1926)

Poems
Letters to a Young Poet

A German poet who reveled in the importance of beauty in the human life, Rilke's *Letters to a Young Poet* is one of the greatest pieces ever written on the nature and necessity of creativity.

———— ♦♦♦ ————

I want to beg you to be patient toward all that is unsolved in your heart and try to love the questions themselves like locked rooms and like books that are written in a very foreign tongue. Do not seek the answers, which cannot be given you because you would not be able to live them. And the point is, to live everything. Live the questions now. Perhaps you will then, gradually, without noticing it, live along some distant day into the answer.

—Rainer Maria Rilke, *Letters to a Young Poet*

———— ♦♦♦ ————

Thomas Mann (1875–1955)

The Magic Mountain
Death in Venice

Mann writes persuasively about the decay that is rotting away our civilization. A writer of immense intelligence and deep philosophical concerns, many consider him to be among the best modern writers.

Jack London (1876–1916)

Call of the Wild

Set in the Great North, this adventure tale of a sled dog and the trials of his difficult existence is a delight for readers of all ages.

Hermann Hesse (1877–1962)

Siddhartha
Steppenwolf
Narcissus and Goldmund

Hesse is capable of both profound symbolism and beautiful lyrical writing. These three books show this combination at its best. *Siddhartha* is the story of the Buddah, and *Steppenwolf* is a fascinating and strange critique of contemporary culture and its values. *Narcissus and Goldmund* deals with the ever-present struggle between reason and passion. All of Hesse's books contain much rich food for thought.

Martin Buber (1878–1965)

I and Thou

This Jewish theologian and philosopher stresses the need to address God and others as a "Thou," emphasizing personal encounter with God and those around us.

E. M. Forster (1879–1970)

A Passage to India

The clash of cultures in British India is the subject of this book. It provides interesting insights into Hinduism and the difficulties posed by British imperialism.

Albert Einstein (1879–1955)

The Meaning of Relativity

Who better to provide a clear explanation of the theory of relativity than the man who formulated it?

James Joyce (1882–1941)

Portrait of the Artist as a Young Man
Ulysses

A vastly original modern writer, Joyce charted a whole new way of portraying reality in literature. *Ulysses* is a very long novel which explores a single day in the life of an Irish man. Immensely influential, though few have successfully attempted to carry the experiment to the lengths he did. A highly cerebral writer, Joyce wrote with a great deal of passion and, at times, a soaring lyricism.

—————————— ♦♦♦ ——————————

History, Stephen said, is a nightmare from which I am trying to awake.

— James Joyce, *Ulysses*

—————————— ♦♦♦ ——————————

Virginia Woolf (1882–1941)

Mrs. Dalloway
To the Lighthouse

Woolf wrote difficult and highly subjective novels which experiment with the stream-of-consciousness mode of writing.

Franz Kafka (1883–1924)

The Trial
The Castle
The Metamorphosis

The nightmarish world of Kafka is unforgettable once you have entered it. He writes of a world without God, where humans are victims of themselves and their deep confusions. If there is no God, ultimately Kafka's vision is right. If there is a God, then he shows us clearly what the gospel rescues us from.

D. H. Lawrence (1885–1930)

Sons and Lovers
Women in Love

A fine writer whose fixation on the necessity of developing the sexual instinct made him a hero to some and anathema to others. Even those who, with me, find his philosophy of life extremely shallow, must admit that he has highlighted many human concerns often ignored by polite society. Lawrence poses many good questions, but mostly arrives at the wrong answers.

Eugene O'Neill (1888–1953)

Long Day's Journey Into Night
The Iceman Cometh

These are powerful dramas about human degradation and despair, which are sure to leave the believer thankful for the hope of the gospel.

Aldous Huxley (1894–1963)

Brave New World

An anti-utopian novel about the nightmare of a plea-sure-driven existence in a not-too-distant future. In fact, with every year that passes, the book becomes more frighteningly relevant.

James Thurber (1894–1961)

The Thurber Carnival

One of the finest American humorists reflects on life and its absurdities with hilarious results. It would be hard to pick a favorite story from this consistently entertaining collection.

F. Scott Fitzgerald (1896–1940)

The Great Gatsby

A novel of love and death in the flapper era, rich in sym-bolism and carefully written.

Erich Maria Remarque (1898–1970)

All Quiet on the Western Front

A gripping short novel which captures the horrors of the First World War. Those interested in further pursuit of this issue might want to read Paul Fussell's fascinating study, *The Great War and Modern Memory*.

Thornton Wilder (1897–1975)

Our Town

Wilder's drama seems simple on the surface but has much to say about the human condition. Readers might also want to try his novel *The Bridge of San Luis Rey,* which is a convincing portrayal of God's superintendence over human existence.

William Faulkner (1897–1962)

The Sound and the Fury
As I Lay Dying

Be forewarned: Faulkner is not easy to read. His richly experimental prose will yield gems to the patient reader, but will be merely an annoyance to those who read primarily for plot. Take the necessary effort, and you will glean much from this master of human psychology. His carefully constructed characters and the Southland that is their home both come unforgettably alive.

Bertolt Brecht (1898–1956)

The Caucassian Chalk Circle
Mother Courage and Her Children

Brecht was an influential political dramatist of the left, whose dramas capture major social and political concerns.

Ernest Hemingway (1899–1961)

For Whom the Bell Tolls
The Sun Also Rises
The Old Man and the Sea

Hemingway's writing is characterized by a spare and unadorned style, a good deal of bravado, and an underlying sense of existential despair. He tells a good story, but his literary reputation has suffered over time. Perhaps his greatest asset is the sharpness of his prose, which he took great pains to make clear, realistic, and free of excessive ornamentation.

Zora Neal Hurston (c. 1900–1960)

Their Eyes Were Watching God

A massively entertaining novel by one of the best African-American writers. Written with the flavor of a folk tale but with very contemporary concerns.

John Steinbeck (1902–1968)

The Grapes of Wrath

Moving story of "Okies" who travel to California in search of a better life, but who do not find the expected promised land.

George Orwell (1903–1950)

1984

Animal Farm

Orwell's powerful writing demonstrates his impatience with the tyrannical tendencies of both the political right (fascism) and left (communism). Both of these two works are frightening, yet show evidence of an underlying sense of the dignity of human beings.

Jean-Paul Sartre (1905–1980)

Nausea
No Exit
Being and Nothingness

Most readers will find Sartre's philosophical writings, such as *Being and Nothingness,* rather impenetrable, but the essence of his despairing and suffocating vision is caught well by his novels. Here is an acute vision of a world without God and without hope.

Albert Camus (1913–1960)

The Stranger
The Plague
The Myth of Sisyphus

Two very powerful novels and a philosophical essay by a French existentialist who called for human dignity and hope, even in an incomprehensible world. Camus is a fine writer and gives the reader much food for thought. Begin your reading of Camus with *The Plague.*

Contemporaries

William Golding

Lord of the Flies

The disturbing tale of a group of young boys who crash on a deserted island and proceed to descend into brutal violence and murder. A telling illustration of the corrupt nature of humanity and of the violence that lies just beneath the surface of human civilization.

Saul Bellow

Adventures of Augie March
Herzog
Mr. Sammler's Planet
Humboldt's Gift

One of the best living novelists in the world today, Saul Bellow's novels are stunningly well-written and filled with intellectual substance. His stories are a feast for the mind, full of provocative ideas and trenchant cultural analysis. They are also full of memorable characters and plot turns that stay with you long after you close the covers of the book.

Ralph Ellison

Invisible Man

A gripping and satisfying novel about a young black man's search for identity in a society where his color makes him invisible. Extremely well-written, with biting realism standing toe-to-toe with passages of heavily symbolic experimental writing. A very fine modern novel.

Gabriel García Márquez

One Hundred Years of Solitude
Love in a Time of Cholera

One Hundred Years of Solitude is a classic novel from South America that falls into the category of "magic realism," an artful mix of fantasy and realism. A long, multigenerational love story by a great writer. *Love in a Time of Cholera* is a moving story of unrequited love and hope that never gives up.

Samuel Beckett

Waiting for Godot
Endgame

Beckett's despairing view of human existence is well captured in these two plays. In a universe without God, characters lead pointless, doomed lives. The plays are saved from ponderousness by Beckett's droll sense of humor.

Thomas Pynchon

Gravity's Rainbow

A bizarre, experimental, but ultimately powerful antiwar novel by a reclusive genius.

Jorge Luis Borges

Labyrinths
Dream Tigers

Borges writes very short stories which are fascinating and curious intellectual puzzles. There is really no other reading experience to which you can compare his work.

Isaac Bashevis Singer

Gimpel the Fool
The Penitent

Singer is a Yiddish writer who delightfully captures the warmth and mystery of Jewish life through the ages. Humor and the supernatural are wedded together for a unique reading experience. His best work is probably found in his short story collections (of which *Gimpel the Fool* is an example), but readers will find treasures amidst all his work. *The Penitent* is a powerful tale of conversion to orthodox Judaism.

Stephen Hawking

A Brief History of Time

Hawking is considered by many to be the most brilliant scientist alive today. Here he muses clearly on what science can tell us about the nature of time and the origins of the universe. Though Christians will be impressed by his own personal heroism and stand to learn much from his book, they probably will not assent to all of his conclusions. Roy Peacock has written a Christian response called *A Brief History of Eternity.*

Thomas S. Kuhn

The Structure of Scientific Revolutions

Kuhn is a powerful tonic for those who believe that science is a completely objective tool for discovering truth. Demolishing the fallacy of logical positivism, he shows how science is dependent upon nonrational procedures and is limited by the prevailing scientific paradigms of its day. A powerful corrective for those who put undue trust in the results of science.

J. D. Salinger

Catcher in the Rye

An infamous book about a young man stifled by meaningless conformity and the shallowness of the values of those adults around him. Salinger captures accurately an adolescent frame of mind. The rough language adds to the portrait of an unhappy young man on a quest for authenticity in a world of "phonies."

Victor Frankl

Man's Search for Meaning

An important work of nonfiction by a psychiatrist who, using his own experiences in a Nazi concentration camp, diagnoses mankind's most basic need as finding meaning in life. Frankl launched a psychological school of thought called "logotherapy," a method with important ramifications for Christian thinkers.

Tennessee Williams

The Glass Menagerie
A Streetcar Named Desire

Williams's dramas are filled with well-conceived characters and an atmosphere of sadness, hopelessness, and despair.

Arthur Miller

Death of a Salesman

A powerful play by one of the most accomplished dramatists of our time. The drama centers on a man trapped in an unhappy and meaningless existence.

Kurt Vonnegut

Cat's Cradle
Slaughterhouse Five

The crazed and absurd universe of Kurt Vonnegut is at its best in these two satirical novels. Vonnegut's kindhearted nihilism is compelling to many readers who cannot make sense of the violent and heartless tendencies of modern civilization. This has made him something of a guru to many—a role he studiously shuns.

Joseph Heller

Catch 22

This hilarious modern classic about the foolishness of war and the weakness of human nature contains some of the funniest passages in modern literature. Here is a novel in which nothing is held sacred.

Edward Albee

Who's Afraid of Virginia Woolf?

A brutal and searing drama about misunderstanding, psychological breakdown, and the "games people play." Fascinating and repelling at the same time.

John Updike

Rabbit, Run

Updike is a fine novelist with a stunningly beautiful prose style. Many of his novels (especially *Rabbit, Run; A Month of Sundays; Roger's Version*) have theological themes which he seems well-equipped to bring off. However, some will find his fixation upon sexual issues rather adolescent and off-putting. When his immense talents are squandered on voyeuristic sexual description, one cannot but lament the waste of his abundant gifts as a writer. His autobiographical *Self-Consciousness* is a personal look at his interests and obsessions.

John Irving

A Prayer for Owen Meany

A very funny episodic novel with an interesting grasp of the providence of God. The stunning conclusion makes this longish novel well worth the effort to read.

James David Duncan

The River Why
The Brothers K

Duncan is a writer of abundant gifts. Though his novels deal with serious issues, they are filled with riotous humor. *The Brothers K* was one of the most moving reading experiences I have had in recent years. This tragic, funny, and profound look at a family whose life is built around baseball, is full of insight into the decade of the 1960s and how it helped to create the cultural environment in which we live.

6

Getting Off to a Good Start:

Great Books for Young Readers

No book is really worth reading at the age of ten which is not equally (and often far more) worth reading at the age of fifty and beyond.

—C. S. LEWIS

The familiar faces of my books welcomed me. I threw myself into my reading chair and gazed around me with pleasure. All my old friends present—there in spirit, ready to talk with me any moment when I was in the mood, making no claim upon my attention when I was not.

—GEORGE MACDONALD

*There is no Frigate like a Book
To take us Lands away
Nor any Coursers like a Page
Of prancing Poetry—
This Traverse may the poorest take
Without oppress of Toll—
How Frugal is the Chariot
That bears the Human Soul*

—EMILY DICKINSON

Great Books for Young Readers

It is never too early to begin to develop a love of good books in children. Mothers, fathers, grandparents, and teachers should all strive to build an appreciation of great reading into young minds. In my earlier book, *Children of a Greater God* (Harvest House, 1995), I give much practical advice on how this can be accomplished, primarily through reading aloud to them from an early age. Here I would like to reprint the list of suggested books which I offered in that volume, along with some helpful annotations.

AGE GROUPINGS:

PS = preschoolers

GS = ages 6–10

YA = young adult

AA = all ages

Note: All these categories are very imprecise and will depend upon the maturity and attention span of your children. They serve only as the roughest guide to the level of difficulty in comprehending the book. Many of the books a child may not be ready to read for himself, but he will be able to digest these stories by having them read aloud. My seven-year-old can listen to and take in any but the most mature books on this list, while other ten-year-olds I know can barely sit still through even the shortest story.

Aesop

Fables

This Greek classic is a collection of very short tales and proverbs which illustrate character strengths and flaws. It is a rich treasure of moral teaching for both young and old. Make sure you get a modern translation as some of the older ones will, by their difficult language, obscure the messages in the stories. [AA]

Louisa May Alcott

Little Women

This was my wife's favorite book as a child, and my two daughters have followed in her footsteps in appreciation of its warm depiction of family life and its unflagging commitment to moral virtue. This book provides realistic yet powerful examples of morality for children and adults alike. [GS/YA]

Hans Christian Andersen

Fairy Tales

Brothers Grimm

Fairy Tales

Two of the classic collections of fairy tales, these include most of the popular favorites. In their original versions they are more violent and less prone to "happy endings" than some of the modern versions of these tales. These stories make good fodder for family discussions of moral values and of how to deal with difficult situations. [PS/GS]

J. M. Barrie

Peter Pan

A charming adventure tale about a young boy who doesn't want to grow up. [GS/YA]

L. Frank Baum

The Wizard of Oz

Dorothy's adventures in Oz make for delightful and imagination-stirring reading. Along the way, we are provided with a powerful picture of the human search to overcome our inadequacies, and a realization that the resources for change are within the grasp of us all. [GS/YA]

Michael Bedard

Emily

Who is this unusual reclusive neighbor who writes poetry? A sweet little tale about a girl who discovers that her neighbor is the famous poet Emily Dickinson. [GS]

Ludwig Bemelmans

Madeline

My two little girls love the rhymed story of Madeline, the little girl who is brave even in the face of having her appendix removed. [GS]

William J. Bennett

The Book of Virtues

An indispensable collection of stories and extracts grouped together by the character qualities they teach. There are hours' worth of valuable material for the whole family contained between the covers of this hefty volume. By all means, buy it and use it. [AA]

Christina Bjork

Linnea in Monet's Garden

This charming story about a young girl who visits the garden of the great painter Monet affirms the importance of great art. [AA]

Michael Bond

A Bear Called Paddington

The humorous misadventures of a lovable, but none-too-bright bear, known for his oversized hat, blue duffle coat, and red Wellington boots. [AA]

Jan Brett

Beauty and the Beast

A good version of the classic tale which teaches that beauty is more than skin-deep and that true love involves sacrifice. [GS/YA]

Margaret Wise Brown

Goodnight Moon

A very simple and soothing book to read to the very young before they go to bed. It seems to produce an environment of peacefulness for the child. [PS]

Jean de Brunhoff

The Story of Babar

The life story of a talking elephant's adventures in France and as king of the elephants. Delightful illustrations. [GS]

John Bunyan

The Pilgrim's Progress

The classic Christian allegory of the spiritual life. The adaptation called *Dangerous Journey* (published by Eerdmans) does a good job of putting the story within the reach of children without sacrificing its substance and power. [GS/YA]

Frances Hodgson Burnett

The Secret Garden
The Little Princess

The Secret Garden is a magical tale about the transformation of an angry and selfish little girl through the healing power of love and friendship. *The Little Princess* teaches the virtues of compassion and consideration for others, even in the face of hardship. [YA]

Sheila Burnford

The Incredible Journey

An exciting tale about two dogs and a cat who brave the wilds in search of their owner. [YA]

Lewis Carroll

Alice's Adventures in Wonderland
Alice Through the Looking Glass

The Alice stories are marked by a seemingly endless supply of wit and invention. They can be thoroughly enjoyed by all ages, but most children will enjoy them more when they are a bit older. [AA]

Susan Coolidge

What Katy Did

A wonderful book that follows the development of character and virtue in a young girl after a crippling accident. [GS/YA]

Barbara Cooney

Miss Rumphius

Miss Rumphius wishes to leave her mark on the world and finds a beautiful way to do it. [GS]

Roald Dahl

Charlie and the Chocolate Factory

A delightful and humorous tale about a young boy whose goodness and decency earn him his dream. His fate is contrasted with those who are greedy, gluttonous, self-absorbed, and disobedient. [GS/YA]

Daniel Defoe

Robinson Crusoe

This is the fascinating tale of a man stranded on a desert island who must learn to survive with his meager store of food and tools. Defoe's tale has explicit references to the sovereignty of God and our need to trust in Him. The story raises many moral issues. [YA]

Tomie dePaola

The Clown of God

The very moving story of a beggar boy who becomes a famous juggler and learns to dedicate his gift to God. [AA]

Charles Dickens

A Christmas Carol

The classic tale of a cruel and selfish man who discovers what is really important in life. *A Tale of Two Cities* is more difficult, but very rewarding. [YA]

Arthur Conan Doyle

Sherlock Holmes stories

Beginning with *A Study in Scarlet,* Doyle wrote four novels and numerous short stories about his fictional detective.

Holmes is a model of how to use logical deductive thinking to solve problems. As a child, I loved to curl up with one of these stories and lose myself in the foggy streets of Edwardian London. The books are exciting as well as intellectually challenging. The vocabulary is sometimes difficult, so they are recommended for older children. [YA]

Clifton Fadiman

World Treasury of Children's Literature (2 Volumes)

Fadiman has gathered together in these two volumes some of the finest children's writing of all time. The set includes poetry, short stories, myths, and selections of longer stories. Both classic and modern pieces are included in this cornucopia of fine children's literature. This is a great place to start building your collection of good books. [AA]

Anne Frank

The Diary of Anne Frank

The emotionally wrenching diary of a young girl whose family and friends suffered at the hands of Nazi Germany. The book teaches valuable lessons about tolerance, loyalty, and the value of human life. [YA]

Don Freeman

Corduroy

An adorable bear finds the home he has always dreamed of. [PS/GS]

Kenneth Grahame

The Wind in the Willows
The Reluctant Dragon

The Wind in the Willows is one of the most charming books ever written, with lovable characters and a deep sense of nostalgia for the innocence and wonder of childhood. Children enjoy its marvelous humor. *The Reluctant Dragon* is a delightful story about a precocious boy and his friendship with a lazy and cowardly dragon. The book provides a good model of how to explore difficult situations and find positive solutions. Its wry humor will make it a treat for adults as well. [AA]

Florence Parry Heide

The Shrinking of Treehorn
Treehorn's Treasure

Sophisticated and wryly humorous little tales about a boy who is always ignored and the bizarre and unexpected things which happen to him. [GS/AA]

James Herriot

All Creatures Great and Small

The first in a series of books about a young English veterinarian in the Yorkshire countryside. [YA]

Russell Hoban

Bedtime for Frances
A Baby Sister for Frances
Bread and Jam for Frances

Wonderful books about a small and rather precocious badger. Children seem to find in Frances a mirror of their own fears, distastes, and faults. *Bread and Jam for Frances* is a good tale for picky eaters. [GS]

Angela Elwell Hunt

The Tale of Three Trees

Three trees each have a dream. One tree wants to become a treasure chest, one a ship, and the third a sign for all mankind. Each of these dreams is fulfilled in unexpected ways by the power of God. A rich allegorical folktale about what God has done for us. [AA]

Hannah Hurnard

Hind's Feet on High Places

This is an allegorical tale about the Christian life, seen through the eyes of Much-Afraid as she goes in search of God's "high places." Valuable for helping young people realize that the life of faith sometimes requires struggle and sacrifice. [YA]

Rudyard Kipling

The Jungle Books
Just So Stories

Kipling's much-loved animal tales teach us a great deal about humans and the way we treat each other. Many good moral lessons and much humorous entertainment await the reader of his stories. [GS/YA]

Charles and Mary Lamb

Tales from Shakespeare

The Lambs manage to capture much of the power and beauty of Shakespeare's dramas in their prose renditions. While no substitute for the bard himself, they are a great introduction to the riches your children can find later in reading the original plays for themselves. [GS/YA]

Andrew Lang

The Blue Fairy Book
The Red Fairy Book

Two representatives in Lang's series of fairy-tale collections. Each book is named after a color. These are the real thing: unexpurgated originals. Be forewarned that the stories do not always have a happy ending and are often a bit grisly. [GS/YA]

Munro Leaf

The Story of Ferdinand

Gentle Ferdinand is a peaceful bull who would rather sit and smell the flowers than fight in the ring. A touching little story. [GS]

Madeliene L'Engle

A Wrinkle in Time

An exciting science fantasy novel with some underlying Christian themes which won the prestigious Newberry award. [YA]

C. S. Lewis

The Chronicles of Narnia [The Lion, the Witch and the Wardrobe; Prince Caspian; The Voyage of the Dawn Treader; The Silver Chair; The Magician's Nephew; The Horse and His Boy; The Last Battle]

A wonderful series of books about some children who find their way into the land of Narnia, where they experience exciting adventures which teach us and them a great deal about redemption, salvation, and the life of faith. These are powerful theological insights artfully cloaked in delightful allegorical tales. Every child should be exposed to the spiritual and moral lessons taught in these classic books. Older children and adults will gain much pleasure and insight from Lewis's space trilogy and others of his many great books. [AA]

C. S. Lewis

Letters to Children

Children who enjoyed the *Chronicles of Narnia* will probably be interested in these letters, many of which discuss the meaning and origin of the Narnian tales. [YA]

Arnold Lobel

Frog and Toad Are Friends

A collection of simple stories demonstrating the power of true friendship. [PS/GS]

Hugh Lofting

Doctor Doolittle

The humorous adventures of a man who "talks with the animals." [GS/YA]

Jack London

The Call of the Wild

This thrilling page-turner chronicles the life of an arctic sled dog. Exposes the thoughtless cruelty of humans and the reawakening of the dog's wild nature. The intensity of the story makes it more suitable for older children. [YA]

George MacDonald

The Golden Key
The Princess and the Goblin
The Princess and Curdie
At the Back of the North Wind
Sir Gibbie

These make good reading as pure fantasy-adventure stories, but on a deeper level they are powerful images of the spiritual life and the path to spiritual maturity. *At the Back of the North Wind* is helpful for children trying to deal with death. MacDonald is a writer of peculiar depth and insight.

Sir Gibbie, one of the most accessible of MacDonald's many novels written primarily for adults, will also be enjoyed by children for its portrayal of a young orphan who learns about his magnificent and unexpected identity. [YA/AA]

Catherine Marshall

Christy

A novel based upon the true experiences of a young woman sent to teach in the Appalachian mountains in 1912. This warmhearted novel is one of several fine books by Catherine Marshall. [YA]

Robert McCloskey

Make Way for Ducklings

A family of ducks face the perils of city life. [GS]

Henrietta C. Mears

What the Bible Is All About for Young Explorers

A great resource for helping children to better understand the Bible, this fine reference work contains overviews of each book of the Bible, themes, outlines, and important background information. Parents be warned: You'll learn a lot too! [GS/YA]

A. A. Milne

When We Were Very Young
Now We Are Six
Winnie the Pooh
The House at Pooh Corner

No child should grow up without a familiarity with the marvelous rhymes and poems contained in Milne's *When We Were Very Young* and *Now We Are Six*. They are charming, disarming, and funny.

The warm and humorous adventures of Winnie the Pooh and his friends are among my all-time favorite books. [AA]

Lucy Montgomery

Anne of Green Gables

Instead of the orphan boy which they had hoped for, a spinster brother and sister are sent young Anne by mistake.

Anne's precocious imagination gets her into (and out of) a number of adventures. [YA]

Mary Norton

The Borrowers

The adventures of tiny people who secretly live in (and borrow from) the homes of the regular-sized. Fun reading for kids. [YA]

Charles Perrault

Fairy Tales
Mother Goose Rhymes

These are undisputed classics that all children are sure to love. [PS/GS]

Watty Piper

The Little Engine That Could

A charming tale which teaches us that perseverance and hard work will pay off, as will a positive attitude toward the struggles which we face in life. [PS/GS]

Chaim Potok

The Chosen

Older readers and listeners will gain much from this powerful novel about the physical, spiritual, and intellectual coming of age of two young Jewish boys. A book full of rich insights and a valuable statement about toleration. [YA]

Beatrix Potter

Peter Rabbit and Other Tales

Peter is an overly curious rabbit who disobeys his mother and almost gets caught by Mr. McGregor. Lovely illustrations highlight these simple tales. [PS/GS]

Howard Pyle

The Adventures of Robin Hood

The exciting adventures of the man who "stole from the rich to give to the poor." [YA]

H. A. Rey

Curious George
Curious George Rides a Bike
Curious George Flies a Kite

George is a monkey who cannot keep himself out of trouble. Unfailingly, he is always rescued by his friend, the Man With the Yellow Hat. [PS/GS]

Barbara Robinson

The Best Christmas Pageant Ever

The story of how the mean and unruly Herdman kids taught the rest of the church the true meaning of Christmas is a fall-down funny book with a powerful message. [AA]

William F. Russell

Classic Myths to Read Aloud

The classic Greek and Roman myths are a gold mine of moral instruction. Russell has written them at a level suitable for young children and has retained their mystery and dignity. These tales make great discussion-starters on moral issues. [GS/YA]

William F. Russell

Classics to Read Aloud to Your Children
More Classics to Read Aloud to Your Children

A valuable collection of excerpts from the classics which should serve to whet the appetite of your children for great books. The entries are age-graded, with helpful introductions and vocabulary guides. [AA]

Maurice Sendak

Where the Wild Things Are

Some parents have found this book about friendly monsters to be an antidote to fear of nightmares. *There's a Nightmare in My Closet* by Mercer Mayer is equally good for this problem issue. [GS]

Doctor Seuss

The Cat in the Hat
Horton Hears a Who

As a child I always had a special place in my heart for the stories of Dr. Seuss. They are a good introduction to the pleasures of language, filled with nonsense and creativity. Many, like *Horton Hears a Who*, teach important lessons. The message "a person's a person, no matter how small" has special poignancy in this day of rampant abortions. [PS/GS]

Anna Sewell

Black Beauty

A good story and a passionate critique of cruelty to animals. [YA]

Margery Sharp

The Rescuers

An adventure story about the brave mice of the Prisoner's Aid Society, who help mice all over the world out of various troubles. [GS/YA]

Isaac Bashevis Singer

Children's Stories

The gifted Yiddish storyteller tells humorous and poignant tales, including the classic story of loyalty, "Zlateh the Goat." [AA]

Esphyr Slobodkina

Caps for Sale

The adventures of a cap peddler whose caps are stolen by mischievous monkeys. [GS]

Patricia St. John

Treasures in the Snow

When her little brother is crippled by the town bully, Annette sets out to gain revenge and learns about anger, hatred, and forgiveness. This and other St. John books are distinguished by powerful Christian messages. [YA]

William Steig

Yellow and Pink

A very funny little parable that makes a powerful argument that humans are the creation of God, not the result of chance or purposeless evolution. Very subtle, very profound. [GS/AA]

Robert Louis Stevenson

A Child's Garden of Verses
Treasure Island

Children of many generations have treasured the simple poems of *A Child's Garden of Verses,* which makes wonderful bedtime reading. *Treasure Island,* a classic pirate tale, is sure to delight most young shipmates! I can remember listening breathlessly to this book as a child, captivated by its exciting twists and turns. [AA/YA]

Adrien Stoutenburg

American Tall Tales

The stories of Paul Bunyan, Pecos Bill, Davy Crockett, Johnny Appleseed, and others stretch our imaginations and our credulity. [GS/YA]

Rosemary Sutcliff

The Sword and the Circle

Brilliant retellings of Arthurian Britain and the knights of the round table. Well-written. [YA]

Jonathan Swift

Gulliver's Travels

Profound and humorous insights into human nature through the eyes of the intrepid traveler, Gulliver. Parts of this book are suitable for children; other sections are best left for young adults. [YA]

Corrie Ten Boom

The Hiding Place

The heroic true story of Corrie Ten Boom and her sister depicts the hardships of a Nazi concentration camp endured by the strength of their faith and trust in God. Though intense in its depiction of evil, the triumph of righteousness makes this very worthwhile reading for adults and children alike. [YA]

J. R. R. Tolkien

The Hobbit, The Lord of the Rings [The Fellowship of the Ring; The Two Towers; The Return of the King], Farmer Giles of Ham

Tolkien's stories celebrate heroism and an appreciation for the simple things of life. They are tales of the battle between good and evil which will excite the listener and challenge the imagination. Tolkien's Christian worldview shows through in subtle and powerful ways. *The Hobbit* and *Farmer Giles* are appropriate for younger children, but *The Lord of the Rings* is more sophisticated, demanding, and possibly a bit frightening for the very young. [YA]

Mark Twain

The Adventures of Tom Sawyer
The Adventures of Huckleberry Finn

These books are among the most entertaining in the English language. You'll laugh and thrill to the adventures of these two intrepid explorers. Books that the entire family will be sure to enjoy. [YA/AA]

Judith Viorst

Alexander and the Terrible, Horrible,
No Good, Very Bad Day

A very funny book that kids (and adults) will immediately be able to relate to. Alexander has one of those days when everything seems to go wrong, and we find ourselves feeling both empathy and humor. A good book for teaching us not to take ourselves too seriously. The kind of book to turn a bad day around and bring a smile to the face of even the most grumpy. [GS/AA]

Walter Wangerin

The Book of the Dun Cow
Potter

Wangerin is a contemporary Christian writer of abundant insight and writing talent. His vocabulary can be difficult at times, but your children will find him worth the effort. [YA]

Rosemary Wells

Morris's Disappearing Bag

One of the many slyly amusing stories by Rosemary Wells. In this one, Morris gets back at his big sisters and brother who tell him that he is too little to play with their toys. [GS]

E. B. White

Charlotte's Web

This wise and eloquent story about the friendship between a pig and a spider is one of the most popular of modern children's stories. White's prose is a model of good writing. [GS/AA]

Laura Ingalls Wilder

Little House on the Prairie series

The nine books of the Little House series are based on the prairie childhood of Laura. They reflect a family lifestyle based on Christian values, hard work, and mutual love and respect. Your children will see moral virtue in action in this fine and unforgettable set of books. Great for reading aloud. [AA]

Margery Williams

Velveteen Rabbit

This beautiful story about a stuffed animal who becomes real through the love of his young owner has become a children's classic. [GS/AA]

Gene Zion

Harry the Dirty Dog

A great story for kids who balk at having to take a bath. [GS]

7

How to Make Use of These Reading Lists

Outside of a dog, a book is man's best friend. Inside a dog, it's too dark to read.

—GROUCHO MARX

In a very real sense, people who have read good literature have lived more than people who cannot or will not read. . . . It is not true that we have only one life to live; if we can read, we can live as many more lives and as many kinds of lives as we wish.

—S. I. HAYAKAWA

When I am dead,
*   I hope it will be said:*
His Sins were scarlet,
*   but his books were read.*

—HILAIRE BELLOC

One of the values of lists such as those contained in this book is that they provide valuable suggestions on which books are worth buying in order to build a personal library of real quality. Many of these books are available in a variety of editions, ranging from the dog-eared used paperback to exquisite leather editions, finely crafted and sturdily bound. Whether your pocketbook dictates frugality or prodigality in your spending on books, such books will be a lasting resource and an intellectual and spiritual treasure. And they are the best of investments in terms of helping you to store up lasting riches of the kind which really matter.

I often refer to my personal library, large and ever expanding, as my "adjacent brain." It is a storehouse for ideas and information, the sum of which I could never manage to stuff into my own cranial cavity. But though I cannot readily draw all this information from my head, it is always as close as my bookshelves. Countless wonders, intriguing ideas, infuriating arguments, paradoxical puzzles, soul-stirring stories, empirical facts, and spiritual resources are all stored on my shelves, and the reach of my hand can bring all of them within my grasp.

But these riches are lost to me if they remain trapped within the covers of unread books. It is not enough simply to own books. They are not meant to be merely looked at, but to be looked into. If we do not read the books we own, we are like the farmer whose land sat over a large reserve of oil buried deep in the ground, but who lived in a tumbledown shanty in ignorance of his wealth because he never made the effort to drill upon his land.

Unfortunately, many people get the idea into their heads that once they are finished with school they are also finished with serious reading, with study, and with learning. For many people, the completion of their formal education marks the end of reading as anything but a leisure pursuit for entertainment. They see reading as an activity akin to watching television—a way to relax and unwind. Books that challenge and require careful reading do not fit this function. Thus, the primary reading material of many Christians is the most predictable sort of fiction or feel-good inspirational writing.

Now there is nothing wrong with reading for entertainment. That is certainly one of its valid functions, and a noble one at that, because many of the very greatest books are extremely entertaining. But if a person reads *only* for entertainment, he robs himself of one of the true pleasures of reading: that of expanding the mind, the heart, the soul, and the spirit.

Learning does not and should not end with the cessation of formal education. Learning is a lifelong activity. God created us to be earnest seekers after the truth our whole lives long; for when we stop learning, we stop growing.

Setting Personal Goals

If we are to seek continued learning, we will have much greater success if we discipline ourselves to bring some kind of plan or structure to this activity. If we do not discipline ourselves and make time for expanding our knowledge and understanding, it is likely that real learning will become a rare commodity. Our lives are simply too busy, too filled with activity, to have a "catch-as-catch-can" attitude toward the acquisition of knowledge and wisdom. If it is not important enough to us to set goals and make thoughtful choices in our reading, we will probably not find the time for serious, focused study. On the other hand, if we do set some achievable and worthwhile goals, we stand to gain much.

One summer while I was still in college, I realized that my knowledge of the Greek and Roman classics was spotty at best, and I decided to focus some of my reading during the summer break on these books. Since my job was during the afternoon hours, and my wife worked mornings, I had an hour or so every day (after feeding and diapering our newborn and doing some cleaning around the apartment) to dedicate to reading. That summer I read Homer's *The Odyssey,* several plays by the major Greek playwrights (Aeschylus, Aristophanes, Sophocles, and Euripides), *The Aeneid* by Virgil, and Plutarch's *Lives of the Noble Greeks and Romans,* as well as a couple of Plato's dialogues and a smattering of Aristotle. Looking back on that summer, it is amazing how much I read and absorbed during those three months. I didn't look forward to starting back to school again because I knew it would get in the way of my education!

To this day, I always try to spend some of my reading time in the classics. Since I always have several books going at once, one is usually a classic, one a work of philosophy or theology, one a devotional classic (for the early mornings), and the others are things that interest me for one reason or another. And I try to finish every book I begin. Sometimes, while forcing my way through a book that is failing to arouse my deepest interest, I will run across a passage that will stop me in my tracks and leave me reeling with its insight. I try to vary my reading between fiction and nonfiction, throwing in an occasional book of poetry or verse. And I am usually reading a number of different books, one after the other, on a subject on which I'm trying to inform myself.

Life is too short not to fill some of the quiet hours with rich reading experiences. I have learned to make time and make sacrifices to bring the insights of some of the most profound men and women into my life through reading quality books.

If you want to start with the cream of the crop, with those books that should be a part of every Christian's "mental furniture," I have narrowed the list down to ten books that will make a very good starting place for your personal reading plan. All of these books have influenced the lives of countless numbers of people throughout history. None of them requires any special knowledge or vocabulary to read with understanding, and all are addressed to the common man, not primarily the theologian or expert. These are a good place to begin, and then you can branch out to explore other classic works.

Ten Books Which Every Christian Ought to Know

1. *Confessions,* Augustine
2. *The Divine Comedy,* Dante
3. *The Imitation of Christ,* Thomas à Kempis
4. *The Practice of the Presence of God,* Brother Lawrence
5. *Pensées,* Blaise Pascal

6. *The Pilgrim's Progress,* John Bunyan
7. *The Brothers Karamazov,* Fyodor Dostoevski
8. *The Pursuit of God,* A. W. Tozer
9. *Mere Christianity,* C. S. Lewis
10. *Celebration of Discipline,* Richard Foster

Here are a couple of other lists to help you expand your reading:

Ten Books to Help You Develop a Christian Worldview

1. *Mere Christianity,* C. S. Lewis
2. *Orthodoxy,* G. K. Chesterton
3. *More Than a Carpenter,* Josh McDowell
4. *The Universe Next Door,* James Sire
5. *Scaling the Secular City,* J. P. Moreland
6. *Knowing God,* J. I. Packer
7. *Christianity for Modern Pagans,* Peter J. Kreeft
8. *Essentials of Evangelical Theology,* Donald Bloesch
9. *The Problem of Pain,* C. S. Lewis
10. *Loving God,* Charles Colson

Ten Authors Who Will Help You Reflect More Deeply on Being a Christian in the Modern World

1. C. S. Lewis
2. Francis Schaeffer
3. Os Guinness

4. Paul Johnson

5. Philip Yancey

6. Alister MacIntyre

7. Reinhold Neibuhr

8. Lesslie Newbigin

9. Walker Percy

10. Ravi Zacharias

Ten Poets Whose Work Demonstrates the Beauty of the Christian View of the World

1. George Herbert

2. T. S. Eliot

3. John Donne

4. Thomas Traherne

5. Gerard Manley Hopkins

6. Luci Shaw

7. Robert Browning

8. Kelly Cherry

9. William Shakespeare

10. John Milton

Ten of My Favorite Novels

1. *The Brothers Karamazov* (Fyodor Dostoevski)

2. *Gulliver's Travels* (Jonathan Swift)

3. *Anna Karenina* (Leo Tolstoy)

4. *Les Miserables* (Victor Hugo)

5. *Jane Eyre* (Charlotte Brontë)

6. *The Brothers K* (James David Duncan)

7. *Huckleberry Finn* (Mark Twain)

8. *The Power and the Glory* (Graham Greene)

9. *The Second Coming* (Walker Percy)

10. *Cancer Ward* (Alexander Solzhenitsyn)

Now it's up to you . . . have fun exploring!

Reading in Groups

As wonderful as the experience of solitary reading and study can be, there is nothing that can compare with the excitement and fun of discussing books we have read with other people who have a similar love for books and reading. Of course, this can and does happen in the most natural ways. On a recent plane trip I was reading Kurt Vonnegut's anti-utopian novel, *Player Piano*. One of the stewardesses, who had recently read the book, saw me reading it and struck up an enjoyable conversation. This kind of thing has happened to me innumerable times. We like to talk with others about experiences we hold in common, whether it is last Sunday's football game, a particularly good movie, a favorite television program, or a good book. Instantly, we have the grounds for an interesting conversation.

Many people have found that such conversations are too good to be left to chance and have formed reading groups with the express purpose of reading and discussing good books. Discussing books with others helps you to cement themes in your mind, to garner new insights, and to share with others the pleasure derived from a truly memorable book.

Discussions in reading groups are similar to the construction of a quilt. Everyone brings his or her own personal insights from a book read in common and shares them with the group. Others see things that you missed or failed to appreciate. Each of us has a unique "pattern" of understanding and interpreting the books we read because each of us draws from a unique fund of experiences and knowledge. We bring our own "square" before the assembled group, and what emerges is a beautiful quilt of enriched understanding. Our own thoughts are stitched together with those of others to form a bigger, fuller, broader appreciation. The quilt takes shape before our eyes in the process of discussion. We see something bigger than we could see when we were limited to our own pair of eyes and our single brain.

This process challenges us to think clearly about the message and meaning of the book under discussion so that we can better articulate it to the others in the group. This encourages us to become more careful readers.

The wondrous thing which happens is that sometimes one member of the group can help others to truly appreciate the riches of a book they just didn't understand. I was called on to lead a discussion of Dostoevski's *Crime and Punishment* for a group I belong to. The majority of those who attended that night had found the book puzzling and a bit tedious. Many failed to enjoy the book or derive much insight from it. But as I brought insights and favorite passages before the group during the course of the evening, a palpable change took place. Suddenly, the book began to make sense to them, and they connected some of their own insights with mine. By the end of the discussion, I had won most of the group over to it. My own connection with and enthusiasm for the book was infectious. Many commented afterward that they left with an appreciation for Dostoevski's profound insight into human nature that they had not had at the beginning of the evening. At other times, I have been on the receiving side of such a discussion, where others have opened up a book for me which I had failed to truly appreciate. It is a glorious demonstration of how the body of Christ can function, even in the reading of a book. Everyone can bring out something that others have not seen and thereby create a fuller understanding for the group as a whole.

The group I belong to currently has about 20 members, with an average turnout of 10 to 15 people at any one session. We meet once a month to talk about the book we have all been reading in common during the previous month. Several have said that the group provides them with the discipline to read many great books they might not otherwise find the time to read.

We laugh a lot. Sometimes we raise our voices in disagreement. Often we share deeply personal experiences which are brought to mind because of the themes of the book.

We emphasize variety in our readings. We have read contemporary novels like Pat Conroy's *Prince of Tides,* John Grisham's *The Firm, A River Runs Through It* by Norman Maclean, *Godric* by Frederick Buechner, Gail Godwin's *Father Melancholy's Daughter, The Second Coming* by Walker Percy, and *This House of Sky* by Ivan Doig. We've read nonfiction such as *Lincoln at Gettysburg* (Gary Wills), Arthur Ashe's autobiographical memoir *Days of Grace, West With the Night* by Beryl Markham, and James McPherson's epic Civil War history, *Battle Cry of Freedom*. We have also discussed children's books such as *Anne of Green Gables* (Lucy Montgomery) and *Wind in the Willows* (Kenneth Grahame). A number of Christian classics have made their way onto our list: *Surprised by Joy* (C. S. Lewis), *Pensées* (Blaise Pascal), *Pilgrim's Progress* (John Bunyan), and *The Imitation of Christ* by Thomas à Kempis.

Many of our very best discussions have come from the classics—memorable books like *Jane Eyre* (Charlotte Bronte), *Frankenstein* (Mary Shelley), *A Farewell to Arms* (Ernest Hemingway), Shakespeare's *The Merchant of Venice*, or from the summer evening when we met in the park to share favorite poems by Hopkins, Blake, Wordsworth, Dickinson, and others.

One of the most valuable things about reading in groups is the discipline it gives you to get through at least one significant book each month. And a reading group will introduce you to many fine authors whose works you'll want to explore on your own. I was so entranced by J. R. R. Tolkien's *The Fellowship of the Ring* that within that year I went on to read everything else he had written.

I have at one time or the other belonged to four different reading groups. The first group, begun while we were still in college by the woman who was to become my wife, became the catalyst not only for our meeting, but also for our learning of common interests in the realm of both books and life. Another group was dedicated to discussing the works of C. S. Lewis and the other Inklings (Lewis's colleagues from Oxford). A third group, made up primarily of clergy and college professors, read academic works in philosophy and theology. The variety of differing theological perspectives made for particularly vigorous discussion. I would encourage you to join or start a group for people who want to read and discuss good books. It is not only intellectually invigorating, it is also immensely enjoyable.

Churches would do well to encourage their members to start small reading groups made up of church members. They might, for example, read some of the books from the great books of the Christian tradition list. Imagine how such reading, held in common, could raise the level of understanding and communication in your fellowship.

Members might also consider that such groups could be a very effective form of evangelism. Nonbelievers who attend can be introduced to the Christian vision of reality in a very nonthreatening and open atmosphere. By reading the right kinds of books, you open people up to consideration of the most fundamental human questions: questions about God, suffering, evil, human nature, redemption, and change. I believe that quality modern fiction can be one of the most powerful ways to open people's hearts to those questions that are only fully answered in the hope of the gospel. For your convenience, I have included a short list of modern novels on these kinds of themes in the Appendix. But keep in mind that these are not all written from a Christian perspective. Some of these books raise the questions only to suggest the wrong answers. But they still do the service of provoking good discussions of important issues. Just make sure you have mature Christians in the group to introduce the answers that arise out of the Christian worldview.

Finally, a few tips on making your group successful:

- Most groups find that once a month is about the right frequency of meeting. A month gives people plenty of time to procure the book and get the reading done. If you make the meeting at a regular time (the first Friday of every month, for example) it is easier for members to plan their schedules around it.

- Keep the group small. Fifteen is about as many as you can accommodate and still have the feeling of intimacy and the opportunity for everyone to have a say. Having too many people seems to raise inhibitions and stifle discussion.

- Have a leader, not a teacher. This is no place for a lecture, and no one person should dominate the group. You need someone to get the discussion going and keep it moving, but this person should allow the discussion to take on a life of its own. The goal is not to find the "correct interpretation" of the book, but rather to discuss and fellowship around the book and its themes. In all the groups I have belonged to, the various members have shared the duty of leading, taking turns in some sort of informal rotation.

- The discussion leader should attempt as much as possible to draw everyone into the discussion. In any group there are likely to be those who will dominate the discussion if they are allowed to. The seasoned leader will learn to draw other people in. I have learned that a valuable discussion technique is to pose a question on which everyone in the room can give their opinion. For instance, during a discussion of *Anne of Green Gables,* the following question was posed: Would you rather be thought beautiful, clever, or good? The responses, as the inquiry made its way around the room, stimulated many interesting comments. The leader should also be aware that some people are simply not very willing to express their opinions aloud. Do not try to force these reticent ones. Over time, their level of confidence will grow, or they will read a book which so affects them that they cannot keep silent.

- It is a good idea for the discussion leader to do a little bit of background study on the author. Sometimes the events of an author's life help to bring insight into his or her writing and to provide a context for understanding and appreciating the work at hand. When I have been the leader and time has allowed, I have read a brief biography of the author prior to the meeting, or other works which might shed light on the book under discussion. If you choose to do this, it is important to keep your remarks short, maybe five to ten minutes. Remember, this is not a lecture, and if you present yourself as an expert on this book or author, it has the effect of making group members feel a lack of confidence that their comments are worth being heard. Nothing damages the spirit of a reading group faster than a "know-it-all" windbag!

- The group I currently belong to sends out a short letter prior to each meeting reminding members of the time, date, place, and book that we are reading. There are also a few questions drawn up by the discussion leader to help us begin thinking about some of the important issues in the book.

- Serving some sort of light snack or refreshments helps to give the meeting an informal and relaxed feeling. Perhaps different members of the group can take turns providing cookies, cheese and crackers, vegetables and dip, or some other snack food. For reasons which I cannot fully explain, the availability of some sort of food seems to relax people.

These few suggestions should be enough to help you get a group started. Even three or four interested readers should be adequate to begin with, and the riches you will gain from participation in such a group are extraordinary. Join the adventure!

God, Human Nature, and the Modern Novel

I love being a writer. What I can't stand is the paperwork.

—PETER DEVRIES

There are three rules for writing the novel. Unfortunately, no one knows what they are.

—W. SOMERSET MAUGHAM

The following novels will make for rich discussion in group settings since they deal with key issues of human experience. Some are written from a Christian perspective; some most definitely are not. Some will contain mature themes which could cause discomfort to some members. Use discretion. But all these books promise to raise important themes for thinking, discussing, and growing.

Bellow, Saul	*The Adventures of Augie March* *Herzog* *Humboldt's Gift* *Mr. Sammler's Planet* *More Die of Heartbreak*
Bernanos, Georges	*The Diary of a Country Priest*
Berry, Wendell	*Fidelity*
Boll, Heinrich	*The Clown*
Buechner, Frederick	*The Book of Bebb* *Godric* *Brendan* *Son of Laughter* *The Final Beast*
Bulgakov, Mikhail	*The Master and Margarita*
Burgess, Anthony	*Earthly Powers*
Camus, Albert	*The Stranger* *The Plague*

Chesterton, G. K.	*Father Brown stories* *The Man Who Was Thursday*
Davies, Robertson	*The Rebel Angels* *What's Bred in the Bone* *The Lyre of Orpheus*
DeVries, Peter	*The Mackerel Plaza*
Duncan, David James	*The River Why* *The Brothers K*
Eco, Umberto	*The Name of the Rose*
Endo, Shusaku	*Silence* *The Scandal*
Ellison, Ralph	*Invisible Man*
Fickett, Harold	*The Holy Fool*
Godwin, Gail	*Father Melancholy's Daughter*
Golding, William	*The Lord of the Flies* *The Spire*
Gramm, Kent	*Clare*
Greene, Graham	*Brighton Rock* *The Power and the Glory* *The Heart of the Matter* *The End of the Affair* *Monsignor Quixote* *The Tenth Man*
Hansen, Ron	*Mariette in Ecstasy*
Heller, Joseph	*Catch 22*
Hesse, Herman	*Siddhartha* *Steppenwolf* *Narcissus and Goldmund*
Howatch, Susan	*Glittering Images* *Glamorous Powers* *Ultimate Prizes*

	Scandalous Risks
	Mystical Paths
	Absolute Truths
Huggins, Byron	*A Wolf Story*
	The Reckoning
Hurston, Zora Neal	*Their Eyes Were Watching God*
Huxley, Aldous	*Brave New World*
Irving, John	*A Prayer for Owen Meany*
Keillor, Garrison	*Lake Wobegon Days*
Lawhead, Stephen	*Taliesin*
	Merlin
	Arthur
L'Engle, Madeleine	*A Severed Wasp*
	A Wrinkle in Time
	A Wind in the Door
	A Swiftly Tilting Planet
Lewis, C. S.	*Out of the Silent Planet*
	Perelandra
	That Hideous Strength
	The Great Divorce
	Till We Have Faces
	The Chronicles of Narnia
Malamud, Bernard	*The Assistant*
	The Fixer
Marquez, Gabriel Marcia	*One Hundred Years of Solitude*
	Love in a Time of Cholera
Mauriac, Francois	*Woman of the Pharisees*
	Viper's Tangle
	Therese
Miller, Walter	*A Canticle for Leibowicz*
Nelson, Shirley	*The Last Year of the War*

O'Connor, Flannery	*Wise Blood* *A Good Man is Hard to Find* *The Violent Bear It Away* *Everything That Rises Must Converge*
Orwell, George	*1984* *Animal Farm*
Pasternak, Boris	*Doctor Zhivago*
Percy, Walker	*The Moviegoer* *The Last Gentleman* *Love in the Ruins* *Lancelot* *The Second Coming* *The Thanatos Syndrome*
Pirsig, Robert	*Zen and the Art of Motorcycle Maintenance*
Potok, Chaim	*The Chosen* *The Promise* *My Name is Asher Lev*
Powers, J. F.	*Morte D'Urban* *Wheat That Springeth Green*
Pym, Barbara	*Quartet in Autumn*
Salinger, J. D.	*The Catcher in the Rye*
Schaeffer, Frank	*Portofino*
Singer, Isaac Bashevis	*The Penitent* *Gimpel the Fool*
Solzhenitsyn, Alexander	*One Day in the Life of Ivan Denisovich* *The First Circle* *Cancer Ward*
Toole, John Kennedy	*A Confederacy of Dunces*

Tyler, Anne	*The Accidental Tourist* *Saint Maybe*
Updike, John	*Pigeon Feathers* *Rabbit, Run* *Roger's Version*
Vonnegut, Kurt	*Player Piano* *Cat's Cradle* *Slaughterhouse Five* *Bluebeard*
Wangerin, Walter	*The Book of the Dun Cow* *The Book of Sorrows* *Ragman and Other Cries of Faith*
Waugh, Evelyn	*A Handful of Dust* *Brideshead Revisited* *The Loved One*
West, Morris	*The Devil's Advocate* *The Clowns of God*
White, T. H.	*The Once and Future King*
Wilder, Thornton	*Our Town* *The Bridge Over San Luis Rey*
Williams, Charles	*War in Heaven* *Descent into Hell*
Wilson, A. N.	*The Healing Art* *Gentlemen in England*
Woiwode, Larry	*Poppa John* *Born Brothers*

Notes

Chapter 1—Discovering Our Christian Heritage

1. G. K. Chesterton, *Orthodoxy* (New York: Dodd, Mead and Co., 1955), p. 85.

2. T. S. Eliot, *The Selected Prose of T.S. Eliot* (New York: Harcourt, Brace, Jovanovich, 1975), p. 38.

3. T. S. Eliot, *The Sacred Wood* (London: Methuen, 1928), p. 52.

4. C. S. Lewis, *Surprised by Joy* (New York: Harcourt, Brace, Jovanovich, 1955), pp. 207–08.

5. In Os Guinness and John Seel, *No God But God* (Chicago: Moody, 1992), p. 199.

Chapter 2—Why Read the Christian Classics?

1. T-Bone Burnett, liner notes to Maria Muldaur album *Gospel Nights*, Takoma Records, 1980.

Chapter 4—Why Read Non-Christian Books?

1. Augustine, *On Christian Doctrine*, II, xi.

2. John Calvin, *Institutes of the Christian Religion*, II, ii, xv.

3. Francis A Schaeffer, "Two Contents, Two Realities," in *The Complete Works of Francis A. Schaeffer*, vol. 3 (Westchester, IL: Crossway Books, 1982), p. 412.

Authors Whose Works Have Been Discussed